1

Peter and Gisela live in Germany. The Second World War is just ending. The Russian soldiers are advancing. Thousands of refugees are straggling along the roads; food is short; children get lost; people are separated from their families. And there is a new frontier between East and West Germany which becomes dangerous to cross.

On their own, Peter and Gisela, from the East, try to reach Düsseldorf in West Germany, where they hope to find Gisela's parents. But will they ever get there?

A BEAM of sunlight fell through a knot-hole in the wall of the barn. Gisela woke up, rubbed her eyes and looked around. She had to think hard for a moment to remember where she was. During the last few weeks she had slept in so many different places, and usually with so many other people in one room, that it seemed very strange to be completely on her own. Then she remembered. She crawled out of the deep hay into which she had burrowed, and stood shivering for a moment in the big, high barn. She smoothed out her coat, carefully removed the straw from it, and went to peep out through the hole. The farmyard lay quiet and deserted in the morning sunshine. A few hens were clucking as they scratched in the manure. There didn't seem to be anyone about.

It was almost a pleasure for Gisela not to be surrounded by a crowd of strangers. She turned towards the little door built into the bigger door of the barn. The hinges creaked as Gisela opened it. It sounded so loud in the stillness of the morning that she became rather alarmed. If there was anyone about, they would almost certainly come to find out who had caused the noise.

But even then no one came. The girl went up to the farmhouse, which was next to the barn, and knocked at the back door. When nobody answered, she went into the house and found herself standing in a room which obviously served as a dairy. Milk churns were arranged in a row on a low shelf, large bowls on a long table, and to the window-sill was fixed a machine for making butter, with which Gisela was very familiar.

Gisela knocked at the first door on the left, still concerned in case one of the occupants of the house was there, and not wanting to appear impolite. But there was still no reply to her knocking, so she continued her exploration.

This was the kitchen. Gisela stopped in the doorway for a moment in amazement. She was suddenly reminded of the story of Snow White and the Seven Dwarfs. It was exactly like that here, a table laid with seven plates and seven forks. But there was one difference. In the fairy-story there were seven small plates, but here there were seven proper plates, the kind grown-ups use.

Nobody had eaten off the plates, and Gisela could easily imagine what had happened. The people who had been living here were just about to sit down for lunch. Then someone had come and shouted that there were soldiers on the way. So they had left everything just where it was and run away. They would almost certainly be back some time during the day. Probably they had hidden themselves in the forest nearby.

On the stove there was a large pan. The fire underneath it had gone out, the heavy coalbucket was half open. Gisela stood on the edge of the bucket, lifted the lid off the pan, and smiled.

Without a moment's hesitation she fetched a fork from the table and began to eat straight from the pan. The appetizing smell had made her feel hungry, and she didn't even bother to look for a serving spoon to put some on to a plate.

Then she had a fright. In the doorway stood a boy.

Refugees on the run

(formerly The Refugees)

Berta Schmidt-Eller

Translated from the German
by Patricia Watson

Scripture Union
47 Marylebone Lane, London W1M 6AX

Alles Wegen Gisela
First published by R. Brockhaus Verlag, Wuppertal, Germany
1962

English translation

First published in England 1968

Reprinted as REFUGEES ON THE RUN 1978

ISBN 0 85421 599 9

Printed in Great Britain by William Clowes & Sons Limited
London, Beccles and Colchester

She had been so completely engrossed in her meal that she hadn't heard him coming.

'Oh! You did make me jump!' She sprang down from the edge of the coal bucket.

'I jumped, too, when I heard a door creaking somewhere here. Was that you?'

'Yes. It was the door of the barn.'

'Did you sleep in the barn?'

'Yes. Do you belong to the house? Where are all the others, then?' She pointed to the table.

'Goodness knows where they are. Away. Everyone is running away. Where have you come from?'

'We've been away from home a long time. It was in the middle of the winter when we had to go away. Mummy and I were evacuated, because Mummy was ill and became worse through the bombing.'

'Oh! Where is your proper home?'

'Nowhere now. In the end we lived on a big farm, much bigger than this one. Mummy used to help a bit with the work, peeling potatoes and sewing and things like that. I helped a bit too, sometimes, taking food to the fields with Doris——'

'Yes, I know—at least, I can imagine. But where are you going now? And where is your mother?'

'Do listen—let me finish speaking, and I'll tell you everything in a minute. It was quite nice on the farm. Then suddenly we were all told to go back home, to Düsseldorf——'

'What? As far as that? How do you hope to get there?'

Gisela stamped her foot indignantly. 'If you don't let me finish, I shan't tell you anything else at all.'

'Oh, don't be cross,' began the boy. 'It's just that I'm surprised that you are completely alone—it's miles and miles to Düsseldorf, believe me!'

Gisela had already calmed down. She had suddenly realized that it was better not to be completely alone after all. She must be patient.

'Well now, listen properly for once, and don't keep

on asking and interrupting. Otherwise I forget what I was going to say.'

'You were about to tell me that you and your mother had to leave the farm.'

'We had our suitcases with us. Mummy was carrying the two big cases and I had the small one. The people said there was one more train and we all wanted to catch it. Mummy couldn't walk very quickly with her cases and she told me to go on ahead with Mrs. Michewski, who had also been evacuated with her children. When we got to the station, the train was already full, but we managed to squeeze ourselves in with the rest. I wanted to wait for Mummy, but I couldn't see her, and the guard insisted we should get in and he pushed me into a carriage. Mrs. Michewski thought Mummy would have been there a long time before and at the end of the train somewhere. We had run right to the front. But Mummy wasn't there, and I didn't find her again. Soon afterwards we had to get out because the train wasn't going any further. I looked everywhere, and called——' Gisela shrugged her shoulders and stared straight ahead.

While she had been telling him all this, the boy had also been reaching into the saucepan with a fork and was eating just as greedily as Gisela had been a short while before.

Now he was looking at the small girl with admiration.

'You seem to be brave enough, anyway. You don't blubber and howl like most girls. What's your name?'

'Gisela, Gisela Fehling. I shall be ten this year.'

'My name's Peter. Come on, let's go on a tour of inspection.'

They went across the hall and came to a lovely dining-room. The furniture was beautifully carved. There was a sofa, and round the table there were high-backed chairs. But Peter wasn't taking any notice of things like that. He didn't even glance at the heavy curtains Gisela was looking at. He went up to the sideboard and pulled out one drawer after the other.

'Empty—they're all empty. They've probably put everything away somewhere for safety. Come on, let's go and look upstairs!'

'If you want to bury the things for the owners, we shall have to stay here till they come back. Otherwise they won't know where to look for them. But I can't stay here for ever. I must get to Düsseldorf somehow, because that's where Mummy will go, and we shall meet again there.'

'You do talk a lot of nonsense,' Peter said, looking sympathetically at her delicate figure. 'Come on, let's go upstairs. Actually I've been through most of the stuff; there was nothing useful there—what I call useful anyway. But the bedclothes are still there—perhaps we could load them on to a hand-cart. Then at least we should have something.'

'But we can't just take things with us! They don't belong to us.'

'They don't belong to anyone now, so it might as well be me who takes them as someone who might come later. That's what you call organization.'

'But, Peter, that's almost like stealing!'

'Call it stealing if you like. I don't care. It doesn't matter what you call it.'

'But it's wrong to steal!'

'Wrong? Even now, when there are no police, and no one knows what belongs to anyone? You're just stupid!'

'It has nothing to do with the police. It's written in the Bible that it's wrong to steal.'

'In the Bible? Do you believe in that book of fairy-tales? I'm not interested in that.'

'Fairy-tales? The Bible isn't a book of fairy-tales!'

'That's what you think! You'll learn when you get older.'

Gisela looked at the boy in complete amazement. They had now reached the first floor. Here they could see that the occupants had gathered together clothes, linen and bedclothes in a great hurry.

'You won't need to sleep in the hay tonight, Gisela! Here is a fine bed and a pillow, and the blankets are up in the attic. I'll bring some down for you. If you only *sleep* in them, that isn't stealing, is it?' He laughed as he said this.

'How long are you going to stay here, then?'

'Until somebody disturbs us. We shall have to wait and see.'

'Goodness! Just look at me!' Gisela called out suddenly. She had walked past a mirror and was looking at herself in horror. Her hair was tangled and untidy, her coat was creased, her face was dirty, and there was a large hole in the knee of her stocking.

'Peter, I must wash my face and comb my hair. And I must darn this hole. If Mummy saw me like this, she wouldn't recognize me. You probably didn't say anything because you look so dirty and untidy yourself.'

'Oh, that doesn't matter.'

'But it *does* matter! We should always wash our faces and comb our hair. Where is the water here? And a bowl? It's easier to wash like that than at the well. They probably haven't got any taps in the house. If I'd seen one I should have remembered sooner that I needed a wash.'

'Downstairs by the back door there are plenty of bowls, if you're quite sure you must wash.'

'In the dairy? But, Peter, those are milk bowls. You can't wash in those!'

'Who knows when they'll be used for milk again? I don't care. All right, I'll bring you a bowl from the bedroom to the pump in the farmyard. But it'll be rather cold washing there.'

'We always had to wash outside, even when it was much colder than this. Sometimes I would rather not have bothered. But Mummy thinks it's dreadful to be dirty. There's sure to be soap in the kitchen somewhere. If only I had a comb!'

'There's bound to be one lying around here somewhere.'

Peter pulled open one drawer after another in the bedroom and eventually found one. There were a few teeth missing, but Gisela said it was better than nothing.

The sun had risen higher now, and the roof of the barn was bathed in sunshine. Gisela took off her coat and dress and began to wash herself energetically. Then she rubbed herself down so vigorously with the coarse hand-towel which Peter had found for her in one of the drawers that she became red in the face and really warm. Her fair hair was so tangled that she tore out whole handfuls of it when she combed it.

'Peter! Peter!' she called, her voice echoing through the house, 'Come outside. You must have a wash, and comb your hair too.'

Peter had no such intention, but Gisela had soon hunted him out, and when she stood in front of him, looking at him so pleadingly, he suddenly felt he had to. He looked down at himself, took off his jacket and, a little hesitantly and nowhere near as thoroughly and vigorously as Gisela, he began the urgently needed wash.

'In the meantime I'll go and look for a clothes-brush. If we brush each other's clothes, then we shan't look so bad.'

Peter shook his head as he watched her go. The things the girl thought of! All this would never have occurred to him. But he felt quite pleased when she cleaned his jacket as well as she could with her small hands, and he took great pains to brush her dress as carefully as possible.

Meanwhile, something else had occurred to Gisela. While she was standing still to let him brush her she said, 'The hens must be fed as well. Look, they are clucking so hungrily and scratching around, but they can't find proper food.'

'I think it's much more important to find food for ourselves.'

'But, Peter, we can't just let the poor creatures starve!'

'Then we'll kill them and eat them.'

'We mustn't do that; they don't belong to us.'

'Belong, belong, belong. You're always talking about things belonging. Nothing belongs to anyone any more. Everything belongs to everyone. What do you think would have happened if we hadn't come? The things would have starved anyway, then. And everything that the people left would have been wasted. It doesn't belong to anyone, or rather, it belongs to the person who finds it.'

'Do you really think so? I don't know—but all the same we can't kill the hens. I know how to make soup but I don't know how to cook chickens. And anyway, who would do the killing?'

'I'd have a go myself—there can't be much to it. They're such little things—not like a pig or a calf. It must be fairly easy.'

The girl looked at Peter, her eyes filled with horror. 'Please, Peter, you mustn't do that. You couldn't help but hurt the hens. When you don't know how to do it properly, it must be dreadful for them.' Suddenly she laughed. 'I'll tell you what, Peter. If we feed them, perhaps they'll lay eggs—that's much nicer. Then we can make omelettes. Yes, come on, let's go and look in the barn and see if we can find food for them.'

Sure enough, in the barn they found a big box of chicken food. It was comical to see how the hens rushed for it, fluttering their wings as they ran, and sometimes stumbling in their haste. They came from every corner of the farmyard when they heard Gisela's calls of encouragement: 'Chookie, chookie, chookie——'

Finally Peter had to tell her to stop. 'That's enough, honestly. You must leave some for tomorrow.'

'But the box is very big, and there are so many of them. Peter, look, they're all terribly hungry.'

'Yes, but there's still quite a lot lying on the ground. Leave them to peck around and find it. I feel hungry again. Are you coming into the house? There must be some food somewhere.'

Peter really had talent when it came to rummaging into all the nooks and crannies. He soon found bread, bacon and sausage, and, in a large meat-safe, some ham and eggs. He cut the bread and covered it with thick slices of sausage. Gisela hesitated before she took some for herself. She put the bread down in front of her, put her hands together, and said, half aloud, 'Lord, bless this food which now we take, and do us good, for Jesus' sake. Amen.'

Peter, chewing vigorously with his mouth too full, stared at Gisela, swallowed, swallowed again, and then finally burst out, 'You really are funny!' He didn't allow himself time to say any more, but he stared at her intently as he went on eating. When he had satisfied his hunger he asked suddenly, 'How do you come to be completely alone? What happened to the people who were with you?'

'I don't know. Yesterday evening, as we were going along the edge of the forest over there, a man came riding past on horseback and shouted something from a distance. I didn't understand what he shouted, because we were in a long line of people, some pushing large or small hand-carts. The old people and the little children were being pushed, but I nearly always walked with the adults. When the man shouted, some of the people tore down their luggage from the carts, others left everything and fled into the forest. There was a tremendous mix-up. Mrs. Michewski pulled her daughter Anneliese behind her and kept on shouting "Hide, hide." I couldn't get across the ditch very quickly, and in the forest there were so many roots and brambles that I tripped and fell, and that's how I got the hole in my stocking.'

'Oh, don't bother talking about the hole in your stocking now!'

'When I'm telling a story you always interrupt!' Gisela looked cross, but then she went on, 'Because my leg was hurting so much I had to rest for a bit. So I crawled into a bush. It was lovely and warm. And after all the calling and shouting it suddenly went very quiet. And I fell asleep. All that walking was jolly tiring, I can tell you. When I woke up I could see between the trees that it was already nearly dark. I shouted, and then I felt really frightened. When I ran out of the forest I couldn't find the main road, but I didn't want to go back into the gloomy forest again. Then I noticed this house, but there was no light in it. The farmyard gate was open, but I didn't go into the house. Instead I went into the barn and lay down in the hay.'

Peter, sitting on the edge of the table, could only burst out, 'Good for you!'

'Well, what are we going to do now?' asked Gisela. 'Will you come with me? I'd like to go and spy out the land a bit.'

They ran across the farmyard into the garden. Gisela wandered happily among the bushes and flower-beds. 'I say, Peter, there'll be berries here later on. What a pity we shan't be staying here that long!'

'Don't shout so loud.'

Peter was having a good look round. Right at the end of the garden he discovered a little gate. He went up to it and nodded to himself. It opened easily. Now they saw that there was a narrow stream running along by the hedge.

'Can you jump across?'

Gisela shrugged her shoulders. 'I don't know. Do you think it's deep? I can swim a bit, but the water is so cold now.'

'Don't risk it then,' said Peter.

Suddenly Gisela shouted, 'Look there, I saw a head!'

Immediately Peter pulled her down and flattened himself on the ground as well. 'Quiet', he whispered. He looked cautiously in the direction in which Gisela had pointed. Yes, he could see the top of a dark head, and next to it, another. Then both heads looked up from the grass. They belonged to two boys, both even younger than Gisela.

'False alarm!' Peter stood up. 'What are you kids doing here, then?'

'We're . . . we wanted . . .' stammered the elder of the two. 'I'm so hungry,' wailed the younger one.

Gisela had got up as soon as she saw Peter do so. 'We've got food; come on,' she called.

'Hey, wait a minute. Don't be in such a hurry!' whispered Peter. 'Later on we shan't have enough for ourselves.'

'But if they're hungry . . .! We only found it accidently ourselves.' Her big blue eyes looked so appealing that Peter could only sigh. 'Have it your own way,' he said.

The four of them went back to the house together. The new arrivals ate greedily. They hadn't said a word to each other in the meantime.

Not until they were full did they explain that they had somehow got separated from a group of refugees. They didn't belong to one another, any more than Peter and Gisela did. The younger boy, who didn't know how old he was, must have been about five or six. He was so weak that Gisela realized they wouldn't be able to take him with them yet. Peter was not at all cross about this. On the contrary. Because of this, Gisela would have to stay longer in the deserted house, and Peter was glad.

2

GISELA HAD taken charge of things in the house. It seemed to come naturally to her. It turned out that one of the new arrivals was also called Peter. Gisela called him 'Peps' to distinguish between them, and this name was adopted by everyone. The younger one was called Heini. After a few days he had quite recovered and ran contentedly round the house, farmyard and garden with the others. If they got too boisterous sometimes, Peter had to warn them not to make so much noise. His eyes were everywhere. In the cellar and in the loft he found flour and corn. In the morning he would bring the eggs from the hen-house, and chop wood and light the fire for Gisela, so that she could do the cooking.

Of course, sometimes the meals she made were rather strange. She knew how to make porridge—the lumps in it were only small ones—and because they had long since finished up all the bread, they had to eat porridge in the mornings. For dinner they had potatoes, with beans or pickled cabbage which they had discovered stored away in the cellar.

'Do you really think we can just take all this?' Gisela hesitated every time.

'Oh, honestly, Gisela, it will go bad if we don't eat it up. How often do I have to tell you? Or do you want us all to starve?' Peter was beginning to get angry.

Whenever they sat down to their meal, Gisela would first give thanks. At first Peter laughed at her, but then Gisela had become angry, and she could get really furious. Her eyes flashed and she even stamped her foot, completely forgetting that her mother had never allowed her to do such things. Whenever she stamped her foot at home, her mother had 'dealt' with her on the spot. But with Peter it was different. As soon as he noticed that she was getting angry he was sorry, and gave in, in the same way as he always gave in when he saw her smile.

Once he said, 'I say, Gisela, you always say in your prayer "What Thou hast given us." So it is God or Saviour, or whoever it is you mean, who gives all this. Or is that just something you say?'

Gisela's eyes immediately began to glint when Peter asked a question like this.

'No, it most certainly is not just something I say! If the owners of the house are not coming back, I really believe that we may eat everything, and that the Saviour has given it to us.'

Of course, it did not always happen that they ate their dinner at dinner-time. The children ate when it occurred to them. Whenever they felt hungry, they would run into the kitchen to see what had become of the potatoes and beans which Gisela had put on the stove earlier in the morning. She knew quite well that beans should be cooked with bits of bacon to flavour them. But, as often happened, while they were out playing in the farmyard or garden, the fire had gone out. Or else Peter, remembering that the last time the beans had been rather tough, had put plenty of fuel into the stove, and the potatoes had boiled to a mush.

Gisela looked sheepishly at the saucepans and unashamedly put the blame on the boys.

'It's your fault. You always fetch me to come and play. I ought to finish the cooking before I go outside with you. Now you must just put up with it.'

But it didn't taste at all nice, and she resolved not to go outside the next day until everything was ready. This resolution did not come to much. Peter, who always swept out the kitchen and helped with the clearing-up after breakfast, pointed out that they had only just eaten, and that it was much too early to start cooking again.

'You can't just sit around in the kitchen all morning. That's pointless. Besides, we need you for the game. It's not so good without you. The kids are much too stupid; you can't do anything really good with them. You can work in the kitchen afterwards. I'll come and peel the potatoes for you and stoke up the fire, and we'll soon have the food ready.'

Gisela didn't take much persuading. The sun was shining, and the thought of romping around outside was much more attractive than sitting in the kitchen. Besides, Peter was perfectly right. It was much too early for dinner.

It wasn't until Peps and Heini suddenly announced in the middle of the game that they were *so* hungry, that the children realized it must be long past midday. The sun had risen high over the barn.

Peter brought in some wood and stirred up the dying embers while Gisela began to busy herself with the saucepans. The younger boys sat on the window-sill looking on.

'Oh, come on, you two; how long do we have to wait before the food is ready? We're starving,' they wailed.

"Well then, you just come and cook it yourselves! You do absolutely nothing, but you expect me to keep on doing the work for you. If you don't be quiet and behave yourselves, I shall come and deal with you.' Gisela meant her scolding to be taken seriously.

Peter laughed. 'How will you deal with them?'

'You're not to laugh at me!'

'All right, Gisela, I'll see that the kids don't get too cheeky. When I deal with people . . .' He looked threateningly in the direction of the window-sill, and that was enough. The two boys disappeared hurriedly.

One dull rainy day, when all four were sitting together in the kitchen, Peter said, 'If anyone comes, we'll just say that we're all one family.'

'But that's telling lies, Peter!'

'Well, what of it? It doesn't matter.'

'Now you're starting again. I hate all this stealing and lying.'

'I know you don't like it. It's because of your Saviour, isn't it?'

The girl nodded.

'Well, I should like to know what He's got to do with it. What does it matter to God or the Saviour if I say that you are my sister? He probably doesn't care—even supposing He's listening anyway.'

'He *does* listen, Peter, honestly. He hears everything and sees everything. Telling lies and stealing make Him very sad.'

'That's only what you've been told, and you believe it because you are still young.'

'Oh, no, Peter, grown-ups believe it too. And our Mishi—but, of course, you don't know who that is. We called him that because Missionary is such a long word. In Sunday school——'

'Sunday school!' What on earth's that?'

'I only had to go to school on weekdays,' Peps interrupted their conversation.

'Oh, it's not at all like day-school. In Sunday school the Mishi told us stories from the Bible. There are stories, but stories of things which really happened, not like Hansel and Gretel. I like the story of Noah's ark—do you know that one?'

'Tell us! Tell us!' shouted Heini immediately.

'It's rather long, but I'll tell it you some time. Then there's the story of how the Saviour changed water into wine at the wedding in Cana.'

'That's impossible, Gisela. Water into wine!' Peter shook his head.

'But it did happen! It's in the Bible. And the Bible is the most important book in the world, and lots of people read it. A hundred thousand Bibles have been printed, or even millions, I'm not sure of the exact number. People read the Bible all over the world, and there are missionaries who go on long journeys on ships and take Bibles everywhere.'

'But people don't speak our language in other countries!'

'Of course not! But then you wouldn't know if you've never been to Sunday school. The Bible has been printed in French and German and . . . and, oh, I don't know, in Chinese, Japanese, African, and all the languages that are spoken in the world. Don't you believe it now? You ought to, Peter.'

Peter stood up. He didn't want to hurt Gisela, but this stuff wasn't for him. It made him feel so uncomfortable.

He began to rummage mechanically in the drawers. The little cupboard where the polish was kept had been spared his investigations until now. Now he pulled out one drawer after another and examined the contents.

'Ugh!' he pulled a face, 'I thought it was something to eat and licked it, and it's soap-powder!'

Gisela sprang towards the cupboard. 'Soap-powder? Oh, fine. Now I can wash your shirts. You needn't pull a face like that, or laugh. I do know how to do it. Over in the barn I saw a wash-board, and I had already thought that if I had some washing-powder I would wash your things for you.'

Soon the kitchen was the scene of great activity. Peter had to drag in a tub and fetch the wash-board. Then the largest pan was put on the stove. All four of them carried water from the pump. Then the boys had to hand over their clothes, and Gisela even put her own clothes into the water too, except for her dress and stockings.

'Peter, you must stoke the fire well, so that the water gets hot quickly.'

The soap-powder was put into the pan, and while the water began to heat up slowly Gisela went to look for pegs.

'Where do you want to hang the washing to dry? It's beginning to rain, so you can't hang it outside.'

Peps and Heini, in the meantime, were trying to build a railway with the pegs, making them travel across the big kitchen table.

'There's lots of room here, Peter. Perhaps you could fix me up a line somewhere.'

'All right, I'll go and see if I can find a line. But what

are we going to eat today? The stove is completely taken up with your washing. Where are you going to cook?'

Gisela clapped her hand to her forehead. 'Oh, how stupid! If only we had some bread!'

'Don't tell me you're thinking of baking bread! That would be the last straw. That would use up the oatmeal and we shouldn't even be able to have porridge for breakfast.'

But Gisela didn't want to bake bread. She wouldn't have had the faintest idea how to set about it.

The younger boys found the washing-party great fun. When the washing was steaming in the large tub, Gisela began vigorously rubbing each item of clothing on the wash-board. Then Peps and Heini discovered the glorious lather.

'Soap bubbles! Let's blow bubbles,' they shouted together.

They ran into the farmyard to fetch pieces of straw, and soon brightly-coloured bubbles were swirling round the kitchen and through the open window.

Peter sat watching the game. After a few minutes he could not resist it. While Gisela was busy scrubbing at the wash-board, the three boys competed with each other to see who could blow the biggest bubbles.

'Oh, Peter, just look at this! Your shirt has fallen to pieces. Now you have no shirt, and it's all my fault,' the little washer-woman called out suddenly.

Peter was unmoved. 'You see, that's what happens. But don't look so mournful. It would probably have fallen to bits by itself before long anyway, without your help. I'll tell you what, let's go and look upstairs. In the attic there's another box full of old things. We might find one there.'

'Aren't we going to get anything to eat today?' wailed the two boys in dismay, when Peter set off with Gisela on this new venture.

'Be patient, you two! If we hadn't come you would have starved to death a long time ago over by the hedge.'

'You mustn't talk like that, Peter. They can't help

being hungry. You'll get something soon, but we must look for a shirt for Peter first.'

Of course the two boys gave up blowing bubbles—they wanted to see what they would find in the attic.

In spite of the rainy weather and the washing, the day turned out to be really pleasant and entertaining. In the box in the attic they found old clothes, aprons, hats with veils and feathers on them, old-fashioned shoes and thick woollen stockings. They were so full of moth-powder that all four began to sneeze violently. It wasn't until it began to get dark that they remembered that downstairs some of the washing was still in the tub, and that they hadn't had any dinner!

Fortunately the fire was still glowing and it was quickly livened up.

'I'll go and see whether there are any eggs, Gisela. Can't you make some pancakes?'

'I don't know. I could try. They really ought to have milk in, I know.'

'Oh, water will do. When are you going to clear away this washing?'

'Just look at the kitchen!' cried the girl in horror. 'If Mummy saw this, I'd get into trouble. If only I hadn't started the washing!'

'Then we wouldn't have found all those lovely clothes. Later on I'll put that new shirt on. It's much better than mine was, only it'll be a bit long.'

Right from the start Gisela had difficulty with the pancakes. The pan which they found in the larder was so heavy that she couldn't really manage it properly. She put an enormous piece of fat into it, then some of the mixture which she and Peter had made. It spat in the pan. Gisela tried to slip a knife underneath the mixture to see whether it was getting brown. She had seen her mother do this, but this mixture was so peculiar. It bubbled in the pan, and Gisela didn't see how she could possibly turn the pancake over.

'You try, Peter; the pan is so heavy.'

'Now I'm supposed to do the cooking as well,' he muttered in comical despair.

He had no success either. The mixture stuck fast to the pan and the fat was swimming round the edge.

'We've done something wrong somewhere. Put some more flour into the mixture. Perhaps it's too thin.'

'No, no! When Mummy did it, it always used to run off the spoon.'

'But you can see that it's not going to turn out right.'

'All right, if you say so.'

Gisela gave in, and stirred in some more flour.

'I shall die of hunger soon,' said Peps.

'You be quiet! You eat and sleep and do nothing all day, and then moan if you have to wait for your food.'

What came out of the pan half-raw, half-burnt, was eaten, but nobody liked it.

'We ought to put sugar on it.'

'Sugar? It's all gone. You would insist on having it on your porridge.'

'I say, Gisela, there's still some jam in the cellar.'

'Oh, yes, jam! You didn't tell us anything about that,' cried Peps.

'As if I needed to tell you!' Peter fumbled in the cellar, and soon came up again carrying a large jar. The contents turned out to be a glorious plum jelly, and it became quite a nice meal after all.

In this way the little household lived happily and untroubled. They slept when they were tired and got up when they woke. They quarrelled and made it up again. If Peter got cross with the youngsters, Gisela soothed him, and if Gisela became annoyed, Peter calmed her in turn. Nobody bothered about them, and they themselves made no inquiries.

It was only in the evening, when they went up to the big bedroom, where they all four slept together, that Gisela would say, almost regularly:

'Peter, tomorrow I must definitely set off and find Mummy. She must have been waiting a long time for me.'

'Leave it a bit. Where would you look for her? You'll get there soon enough. One of these days I'll go through the forest across to the main road, and see how far they've got with the war. We'll be all right here for a long time yet.'

Gisela seemed satisfied with this. But that was mostly because she was much too tired to argue.

Before she closed her eyes she would put her hands together and fall asleep as she prayed for protection during the night.

Peter seldom fell asleep so quickly. When he heard the regular breathing of the boys and saw Gisela lying curled up in her bed, he opened the window quietly and listened into the night. The sky stretched like dark velvet over the house and forest. A bat flitted past and startled the boy. The wind rustled the trees gently. There was no shooting, no shouting, nothing. Had they been forgotten by everyone? Had the war passed this house by? Would nobody disturb their peace? How long would they be able to stay?

At some point the girl would have to go back to her mother. Where could she be?

Peter thought of his mother. And of his little sister. He felt a piercing pain in the region of his heart, and closed his eyes. But the picture, that dreadful picture, stood all the more clearly in front of his eyes.

He pressed his lips together. He wanted to cry, but only a groan came out. He mustn't think about it. He mustn't think about it.

He turned back into the room. Gisela, little merry Gisela. His little sister had been just as sweet and merry. Sometimes just as quarrelsome and cross as well. But now?

No, nothing must ever happen to Gisela. He had no one besides her. He would take her home. Perhaps, if he succeeded, he would be allowed to stay with them. With Gisela's mother. If he told them what had happened to him and his mother and sister. Once again he could see the cruel pictures in his mind's eye. He stretched himself out on his bed, and finally sleep overtook him.

3

None of the children, not even fourteen-year-old Peter, could have said later how long their stay in the deserted farmhouse lasted.

Gisela and the younger boys were completely carefree. Except for the question of when they would set off for home, Gisela had no problems. And the boys found this sort of life exciting, and were very glad that Peter managed to keep on persuading Gisela to stay a bit longer.

Sometimes he had to use all his powers of persuasion. In the evening it was easy, but when the question was raised in the day-time—usually it was something to do with the running of the house which caused Gisela's mother to be mentioned—Gisela could get quite het up. She would stand in front of Peter, her eyes bright and her fists clenched, and say to him angrily, 'Peter, you *must* tell me when we're going. If you don't want to take me, I'll go alone—yes, alone! And then it will be your fault if anything happens to me and I get lost!'

'Be patient, Gisela. Please be patient. Of course I'll take you, that's for certain. But be reasonable. The war must be over first.'

Such episodes were rare. Peter kept to himself the fact that he was secretly very worried, and that again and again a great fear rose up inside him, sometimes even in the middle of a really good game.

One day he dragged two planks of wood from the wood-shed to the little gate at the end of the garden. When Gisela questioned him, he gave a vague answer.

In the meantime the stock of sausage and bacon was becoming noticeably smaller. Peter warned them to use only a little at a time. Gisela realized the need for this, but the younger boys grumbled. Then Peter became so furious that Gisela cried in horror.

'Peter, Peter! I'm afraid of you! Don't get so angry!'

He became calmer then, but when Gisela wasn't looking there were several cuffs on the head for Peps and Heini. 'If you so much as breathe a word to Gisela that I've hit you, I'll put you in the cellar and leave you there to starve! You ought to be jolly thankful that we took you in at all.'

At threats like these the two became subdued and silent. But they didn't feel any particular affection for Peter.

Then one sunny afternoon there came a sudden change in the situation. It meant the end of the carefree days in their forest-farm.

They were playing hide-and-seek in the big garden. Gisela had found a very good hiding-place and was certain that Peter would only find her after a long search. They had arranged a 'den.' Whoever had been seen had to run as fast as he could to a certain place and call out three times, 'One, two, three, I am free.' But if the person who had seen him reached the 'den' first, then he had to shout, 'One, two, three, Gisela seen,' or Peps or Heini, whoever he had beaten. The person who was beaten had to be on next time.

For a long time Gisela had been trying to work out the quickest way to the lime-tree in front of the kitchen window. That was the 'den.' She would have to run between the bushes and trees to beat Peter to the spot. She was looking forward to the fun. Then Peter came running towards her. But he must have seen Peps. Why didn't he run to the 'den'? Now he had found Heini. Gisela wanted to beat them all, so she jumped out of her hiding-place and ran across the lawn towards the house.

Then she heard Peter panting behind her, and his running footsteps. She was just about to let out a cry of triumph when she felt herself seized by her dress so violently that she lost her balance and fell over. She fell so heavily that she cried out with pain and tears welled up in her eyes.

Then Peter's face was over her. He pressed his hand over her mouth, and he had in his eyes the expression which made Gisela feel afraid.

'Quiet! Quiet!' he said. '*They're* there!'

Gisela didn't know who 'they' were, but she sensed that Peter saw danger. It reminded her of what it had been like during the weeks when they had been escaping. She had almost forgotten. But she grasped immediately that she must follow Peter.

'Stay lying here! You can't be seen from the house through the bushes. I'll come for you in a minute.' Peter had whispered this urgently. Now he half-crawled, half-jumped, from bush to bush, from hedge to hedge. He must have already warned Heini and Peps. Gisela lay flat on her stomach, and when she lifted her head a little, she could see three small figures hurrying towards the little gate at the end of the garden, bending low and using the bushes for cover.

The small girl was so scared that she forgot the pain in her foot which had developed after her fall.

'Dear Saviour, help us, and don't let anything happen to Peter,' she prayed.

Suddenly the boy was back.

'I didn't see you coming.'

'Shhh! Come with me and keep down!'

Gisela followed Peter's instructions as well as she could. Now she could hear the noise of voices and singing coming from the farmyard. 'Have the people from the house come back?' she asked in a whisper.

Peter shook his head. 'Soldiers.'

'Well, then, I'm not really afraid. They wouldn't do *me* any harm.'

Peter gave her a look, and she was silent.

Now she found out what Peter had had in mind with

the planks. They were lying across the stream behind the hedge.

'You can walk upright here. They won't see us.' The boy's voice trembled with anxiety. Peps and Heini were already waiting on the other side.

'Is that why you brought the planks?'

He nodded.

He led them a short way along the other side of the stream, after he had given the planks a hefty kick and caused them both to fall into the water and float away downstream.

'But Peter, now we shan't be able to get across again.'

'We shan't want to either. And we don't want them noticing straightaway that we're over here. They'll see that someone has been in the house. It's quite likely that the fire in the stove is still glowing. If they begin a search . . . it's much better that the planks should not be there.'

'You think of everything, Peter.'

He stopped at a hollow tree. 'You can all three crawl into there. Sit still and keep quiet. Leave the branches covering up the entrance, then no one will see you. I'll be back soon. But you must be quiet. Do you understand?'

'Where are you going then?'

Peter didn't answer. He had discovered this hideout several days before and had laid his plans very carefully. Now they had to be put into operation. He had cut a number of branches with his pen-knife and placed them in front of the opening in the tree.

Then he ran back, jumped across the stream and hurried, half-stooping, half-crawling, as before, towards the house. As his footsteps died away Heini was the first to speak. He only whispered, but his tone was rather sulky.

'Why doesn't he stay here? He's probably gone to eat ham and sausage, and we shan't get anything.'

'Be quiet, Heini! You say hateful things. Peter might manage to get something for us on the way, if only he isn't caught. Come on, let's pray by ourselves. Because the Saviour hears, even if we only pray silently.'

'Pooh!' said Peps.

'Yes, He does hear. I know for certain.'

'Peter laughs about it all.'

'Don't speak so loudly!'

'Not long ago, when you were in the kitchen preparing the food, I asked him whether all that stuff about the Saviour was true, and whether He does hear when you pray to Him in the evening, and Peter just laughed. So you see, that's what he's like. But you're always on his side.'

'Peps, you're—I don't know what you are! In any case, you're not nice. Especially when Peter has gone to fetch things for us, even though the soldiers are there. What else do you suppose he's doing?'

'Oh, yes, he'll probably bring something for himself and you.'

Heini joined in the conversation now. 'They've always been nice to us. That time when I couldn't walk any further, and always.'

'Well, you were the first one to say that he'd gone to fetch sausage and ham for himself.'

'Only because you're always saying it.'

'Don't let's quarrel now. You can go and find out what he's doing if you like, but you wouldn't dare. *I* would dare, but if Peter says we should stay here, then that's the best thing to do. Besides, I want to tell you something. I believe that the Saviour has sent Peter to us specially so that he can help us. None of us could have jumped across the stream, and Peter put the planks there some time ago. Peter is kind and clever, and lots of other things as well.'

'Yes, he's always nice to you, because he likes you. We like you as well. And you think he's good and everything because you like him. But he never cuffed you.'

'Did he do that to you, then?'

'Yes, and he was going to lock us in the cellar if we told you. He was going to let us starve! But now he hasn't got a cellar to lock us in. Now perhaps the soldiers will lock him in the cellar and let him starve!'

'You say some awful things, Peps! I didn't know anything about this. Why did he cuff you?'

'Just because he felt like it. And as far as I'm concerned he needn't come back again.'

'Oh, you dreadful boy! What would become of us if Peter wasn't with us? He's going to take me back to Düsseldorf. Do you know how far that is? You'd have to travel at least three days on a train—or two anyway.'

'And you are hoping to walk that far? He'll never do it. He's just saying that!'

'If only he'd bring some food! I'm starving.'

'There you are, you see. Today at dinner you wouldn't eat the potatoes because there wasn't enough bacon with them.'

'I want to get out of here. Let's just go and see if he's coming.'

'Oh, do be quiet. He'll be here soon.'

The shadows of the trees along the bank were growing longer and longer. A cool breeze was blowing across the stream. The children sat huddled together in the tree and peeped out at the spot where they had crossed the stream before. The youngest fell asleep with his head against Gisela. Peps was silent. The girl sat with her hands folded. The boy stared at her as she moved her lips without making a sound.

'She's praying again,' he thought to himself, and found comfort in the thought.

Darkness fell. In a treetop a blackbird was singing its sweet melodious song.

4

PETER REACHED the house without being seen. From the room with the fine furniture came the sound of laughter and chatter. He crept up the stairs to the first floor. He wanted to fetch a pillow and blanket for Gisela. Who could tell where they might have to camp on future nights?—in forests, barns, or under the open sky somewhere. At least she would have a pillow under her head and a blanket to keep her warm. It was always cold at night.

If only he could take something to eat as well. But to do that he'd have to wait until it was dark.

Footsteps on the stairs caused the boy to freeze. Then, with one bound, he was under the bed. He crept right to the back by the wall and drew in his legs. The crunch of heavy boots came nearer. The door was kicked open.

Peter's heart thumped. Would they discover him? Would he still have an opportunity to grab a blanket and pillow before he ran away? In and out, out and in, went the legs as he watched them from his hiding-place.

Now the men appeared to be at the cupboard. Clean linen fell to the floor, but no one bent to pick it up. Two, three, four boots trod on it. The room was filled with voices and laughter. Then it was suddenly empty again.

But now the footsteps and voices were in the room next door. Peter remained motionless. The minutes seemed like eternity to him. How was he to get out of here? Wait until it was dark? Would the three left behind in the hollow tree wait patiently until he returned?

Gisela was sensible enough. But the kids? She would

have trouble with them. With Heini, always hungry and impatient, and with Peps, who was not much better. When evening came and there was nothing to eat what would they get up to then?

In the meantime, the house had become quieter. There were only faint sounds of talking and singing from downstairs.

Slowly and carefully Peter edged his way to the front of the bed and listened. But there was nothing. Probably they were all downstairs eating and drinking by now. In the cellar there was wine. Peter had never touched it. He didn't like wine, and it wouldn't have done the others any good.

Peter tore a blanket from the bed and ran into the bedroom next door to fetch a pillow. The feathers flew everywhere. The pillows had been slit open and were completely useless. Peter clenched his teeth with anger and disappointment. He racked his brains quickly. Up in the attic there were other bedclothes. Perhaps there was a pillow up there that he could use for Gisela.

With the blanket under his arm he pushed open the door, and straightaway collided with a very tall man.

They both let out a cry. One was a howl of triumph which quickly brought the other soldiers like a pack of hounds. The other was a cry of fear and anger. Peter hit out, bit, scratched and kicked.

All to no purpose. Two, four, six fists seized and hit him. A red stream of blood poured from his nose. Then he lost consciousness.

When he woke up, the moon was shining brightly. He tried to get up, and immediately groaned with the pain. He could feel moist and sticky blood over his neck, face and hands. Every limb ached.

Gisela! The thought shot through his head.

How long had he been lying here? It was already night-time. Would Gisela still be waiting in the tree across the stream? Would she be afraid? Would she be crying? And the boys? Would she be able to manage them without him? No blanket, no pillow, nothing to eat. And he beaten up into the bargain.

Was he to return empty-handed?

The house was remarkably quiet. The moonlight was streaming in at the windows.

In spite of his pain, Peter moved cautiously towards the back door. Nothing stirred. Beneath the kitchen window chicken feathers were strewn about, and chickens' heads. He remembered how Gisela had protested when he had mentioned killing them. 'You couldn't help but hurt the hens,' she had said, or something like that. Peter stood up cautiously and peeped in through the kitchen window. On the table he could see bottles—almost certainly empty. And there, in the middle of the table, the remains of a piece of ham.

That he must have!

Flattening himself against the wall he crept into the house. He fumbled around the kitchen in the dark. A handle! He moved it back carefully, his heart thumping. Success! He went into the hall. The moon shone brightly, lighting up the staircase. If he crept up quickly perhaps he would be able to get a blanket and pillow for Gisela after all!

On the first floor he trod on something soft outside one of the bedroom doors. He fumbled and picked it up. It was a blanket. Marvellous, now he wouldn't have to go in. It must be the blanket he had dropped when he was caught.

Should he risk going up into the attic to fetch something else? A pillow? Or into the room next door where he knew there was some flour? They needed anything he could get now.

Very quietly, step by step, he crept up. He started when one of the stairs creaked under his foot. He held his breath and listened. But there was no sound, the house was silent.

He went on. The attic door was open. He knew exactly where to find the box full of bedding. His heart raced.

Was someone coming up the stairs after him? He ducked down behind a box and listened. The blood rushed to his ears.

All this for your sake, Gisela. There was the box. He reached into it. There was a pillow there. Quickly Peter wrapped the pillow and the remains of the ham in the blanket, and crept downstairs. He breathed a sigh of relief when he quietly pulled the back door shut behind him. Keeping first close to the house, then in the shadow of the barn, he reached the garden. As he jumped across the stream, his strength failed him. He was just able to throw his bundle on to the opposite bank before he fell into the water. Soaked up to his armpits, he clambered on to dry ground, recovered his breath a little, and staggered to the hollow tree. Bending back the branches, he could see in the pale moonlight the three sleeping peacefully. Exhausted, he sank to the ground near the tree.

5

GISELA'S VOICE woke Peter out of his uneasy sleep.

'Oh, Peter, Peter! What has happened? What have you done? You're covered in blood!'

Her anxiety and concern did him a world of good. Slowly he got up.

'It's nothing, Gisela. I went to fetch a blanket and a pillow, and something to eat as well.'

'Food! Give me some! I'm so hungry!' That was Heini, of course. But he was silent immediately when he climbed out of his hiding-place and saw Peter. What had happened to him?

Tears were rolling down Gisela's cheeks now.

'Hey, what's the matter? Don't cry!'

The girl dried her tears with the large apron which she still had on from the day before.

'Come on, Peter, let me help you. We must wash the blood off. Does it hurt very much? You were away such a long time.'

Gisela's words came with a rush. Peter let the torrent of questions flow. How kind she could be, this little Gisela, who was sometimes so obstinate and quarrelsome.

They went to the stream. Gisela helped him and rubbed the blood from his jacket with a dampened corner of her apron as well as she could. But there were still a lot of dark stains.

'There's some blood here on the blanket. A large patch on the edge. Couldn't I wash that bit?'

'Oh, leave it,' he said. 'It's not all that important. We must get away from here. If the soldiers in the house wake up and find me missing. . . .'

'But I'm hungry! Yesterday evening there was nothing

to eat, and now we've got to start walking. I just can't, when I'm as hungry as this!'

Peter didn't answer. He looked carefully in all directions. The sky was grey and heavy.

'Just be quiet for a while, Peps and Heini! First of all we must get away. If anything happened to Peter, how would we manage on our own?'

She turned to Peter. 'Come on; we'll go a little way along this path away from the house. Such a pity! Our lovely house! But now we'll go straight to my house in Düsseldorf, and not stop anywhere else. Do you agree, Peter?'

'Well, we must get away. But we can't go along the path by the stream. I'm just trying to remember where the sun rises.'

'Well, if you're going to wait for the sun,' said Peps, 'then we've got time for food. With weather like this the sun won't be here for ages!'

Peter wasn't listening.

'It's like this, Gisela,' he explained, ignoring the younger boys. 'I must know where the sun rises because that is the east. But we want to go west, so we must go in the opposite direction. Do you understand?'

'If you say so, it must be right. But how do you know?'

'We learnt it in school; at least, the bit about east and west. But you ought to know that Düsseldorf lies in the west. West from here, anyway. And in the west of Germany.'

'Hm. I don't really know. Perhaps we did learn it in school and I've forgotten. But it doesn't matter, as long as you know. You will take me home, won't you? I'll never find it alone. And I haven't a clue about the sun.'

'Gisela, yesterday you said it would take several days by train. Are you hoping to walk? You'll never make it!'

Peter threw Peps an angry glance, but said privately to Gisela, 'Don't be afraid, Gisela. I'll get you there somehow.'

'But we must take the boys with us. They haven't anyone besides us. And that reminds me, you shouldn't cuff Heini and Peps just because you feel like it.'

'Have you been telling tales?' Peter glowered at the boys.

'We were talking about it yesterday when you were such a long time away. We didn't mean to tell.'

'I see, you didn't mean to tell. You were probably thinking—now he's gone away and won't come back again, we'll split on him. I know you. You just wait!' He turned his back on them and looked at Gisela. 'You must believe me. It's not true that I did it just because I felt like it. Only when they were cheeky, or moaned about the food, or got into some kind of mischief. Apart from that, I haven't ever hit them. But when I do cuff someone I do it properly!' He looked at the boys over his shoulder. 'You're going to notice that more often in future!'

He picked up the bundle and said shortly, 'Come on, let's go. In the mornings the sun was always opposite the barn, so we know which direction to take.'

So the four of them trotted off across the meadow into the grey morning.

Soon they came to a track which led to a main road. But Peter was not sure that this was the right road. He looked carefully in all directions.

Then Gisela asked whether they could have something to eat now. Peter nodded.

'We can sit over there by the hedge.'

They ran across the field and sat down in the grass by the hedge. They were on the edge of a large cabbage-field. There was a smell of half-rotten cabbages.

Peter took out his penknife, cut one of the cabbages, and stripped off the outer leaves.

'Are we supposed to eat that?' asked Peps, and immediately received a thump from Peter.

'You'll eat what you get and be thankful. Understand?'

'But you said you'd brought food with you!'

'So I have.' Peter unwrapped the ham. 'That's for Gisela.'

'No, Peter. We'll share it. Otherwise I shan't eat any of it. I like eating raw cabbage. I should never have guessed that the inside was so white.'

So they shared, ate, and then began walking again. They walked through forests, past fields and along narrow tracks, and only saw the roofs of farmhouses in the distance among the bright green branches of young trees.

Heini was the first to complain that he couldn't walk any further.

'Oh, you are a nuisance!' grumbled Peter.

Gisela, who had also been wishing they could walk more slowly, took Heini's side.

'I don't think I can walk any further either, Peter. Let's have a rest. It will soon be evening, and we've been walking all the time. Can't we stay over there by the barn?'

'Evening? That's what you think! Evening's a long time away. If we only walk this far every day, we'll never get to Düsseldorf. The winter will be here again, and what shall we do then? If Heini hadn't begun to moan, you wouldn't have said a word. You always side with the boys.'

'But, Peter, the winter is only just over. We shall get home all right. We're not used to walking yet. I'm not going any further than to that barn today, so there!' Gisela tossed her head defiantly and trotted across the field to the barn.

'Obstinate turkey!' Peter shouted angrily, and ran on ahead without turning round. But at the barn he stopped and waited until the other three had caught him up.

Gisela had been a little afraid of what might happen. Now she was pleased that Peter had given in.

She had a look round. There was an open rack on which carrots had been stored for the winter.

'Peter, look! Here are lots of carrots. Now we've something else to eat.' She looked appealingly at him. 'Don't be angry any more. Tomorrow we'll walk for hours and get a really long way.'

Peter just shrugged his shoulders, threw himself on to the hay, wiped the worst dirt from one of the carrots, and began chewing.

6

THE NEXT morning, the first thing Peter did was to leave the other three behind in the barn. 'I just want to go to that village over there and keep my ears open to find out what's happening. We've no idea what's been going on while we were living undisturbed on the farm.'

The younger boys were content. If Gisela stayed with them, they didn't worry. They munched one carrot after another, and romped with Gisela in the small amount of hay that was there.

It was quite a time before Peter came back.

Gisela looked at him expectantly.

'The people say the war is over,' Peter reported. 'But there are foreign soldiers all over the village.'

'What are we going to do, then, Peter?' Gisela looked anxious.

Peter bent down, rolled Gisela's pillow in the blanket, and moved off into the field. The younger boys nudged one another. When Peter wore an expression like that, it was better not to argue or ask questions.

Gisela kept pace with Peter. 'Shall I go and ask whether someone in the village would give us food?'

'Better not—it's best to try and manage on our own.'

'But I'm not afraid to, Peter.'

'That's all very well. Where do you think you're going to get anything? That's just it. Somebody will have to . . . well, I'm not begging anyway!'

'What will somebody have to do?'

Peter was silent and bit his lip.

'I can imagine what you mean, Peter. You were going to say "organize," weren't you?'

The boy nodded. 'Yes, you see.'

'But there isn't an empty house now. You can't say this time that things will go bad, and that's stealing, Peter.'

'Well, even if it is stealing, we've got to get food somehow.'

'Let Peter get on with it, Gisela,' advised Peps.

'No, we can't do that. We mustn't. I'd rather go to the people myself and tell them about our difficulties. Perhaps they'd give us food then. They'd be sure to give us something.'

Slowly they approached the village. Peter stopped near some bushes.

'Come on, Peps. We two will go into the village. Gisela can wait here with Heini.'

'Peter!'

'I know what you're going to say. You needn't worry. What I'm going to do will be all right.'

Gisela watched the boys go.

'What are we going to do, Heini? Peter could easily have taken us with him.'

'He doesn't want us to see what he gets. Or perhaps he's going to steal after all.'

'You mustn't say that, Heini. It's got something to do with the soldiers. But I'm not afraid. They wouldn't do anything to us if the war is over.'

It was quite still. The sun shone warmly and larks were singing high up above. Gisela shaded her eyes with her hand and looked into the blue sky.

'Just listen to that lark, Heini! Isn't it lovely! That's how I should like to sing—loudly and happily. It's such a lovely day.'

She looked around. 'And flowers everywhere! Come on, let's pick a big bunch.'

She jumped up and began picking the flowers in the field. But then she stopped.

'I suppose,' she said slowly and sadly, 'there's no point in it. We can't take them with us. We haven't a vase anywhere, and they'll just die if we carry them around in our hands. What a pity!'

'I say, Gisela, do you really think Peter can take us to your home?'

'Of course; why not?'

'Even when it's so far? Do you think we're still going the right way? How does he know?'

'If only I knew what he was doing in the village! Come on, let's go and see. I don't like just sitting here waiting for him.'

Heini was ready to go at once. They went along the same path as Peter and Peps and quickly came near the village. Then they heard the rattle of carts behind them.

'I say, Gisela; there are Russian soldiers coming! Where can we go? There's nowhere to hide!'

The girl felt her heart begin to thump. They were quite close to the first house in the village.

'Run, Heini!' She pulled him by the hand and they ran towards the house.

Then, just in time, Peter came round the corner. He grasped the situation straightaway and ran over to them. The tramping of horses came nearer and nearer, and the children darted across the street and in at the garden gate. Peter pushed Gisela into the house and quickly closed the door.

'What's all this? What's going on here?' called a voice from a room at the back.

Peter, still out of breath, gasped, 'Soldiers!'

'Are you so scared, you poor things? But the war is over; you needn't be frightened. They won't hurt you.'

'There you are, Peter. That's what I thought.'

'Come a bit nearer.' The old man who had come forward from the dark end of the hall asked them more questions, and then pushed them into the little kitchen. A bent old lady was busy at a stove.

She listened to the children's story and shook her head.

'We haven't much to eat either,' she explained, 'but I

will make you some soup. In the meantime you can have a rest.'

They sat down on a seat in the garden, and now Peter had his first opportunity to find out what Gisela and Heini had been doing in the village.

Rather subdued, Gisela told him that she had got tired of waiting.

'Don't ever do anything like that again. You must promise, Gisela.'

'Well, then, you must promise me something as well.'

'What?'

'That you won't steal when you go into the villages, or tell lies, or "organize." That's the same as stealing, anyway.'

'But "organizing" is something quite different.'

'Oh, no, it isn't; it's exactly the same, and you must promise me. Otherwise I shan't promise you anything.'

'All right, I promise you. But only if you keep your promise and don't just do the first thing that comes into your head while I'm spying out the land.'

'All right, I promise you that I will never run away, but always stay where you tell me.' Gisela stood up and solemnly held out her hand.

Peter looked at her in astonishment, but she was quite serious about it.

'Now you promise me too, Peter.'

'All right.' Peter took a deep breath. It was an awful lot to have to promise in return.

'I promise you. . . .' Peter stood in front of Gisela and shook his head. 'No, it's not fair. Your promise is only a little one. Why should I have to promise something so big?'

'Come on, you must promise; otherwise mine doesn't count either. Now say it—and remember, we must keep them afterwards.'

'Keep them—that's just it. You think it's all so simple. Not to tell lies—but you can't keep a promise like that for ever. There are bound to be times when I shall have to tell a lie.'

'You were about to promise just now—and you have half promised already.'

'Yes, but that was before I'd thought about it. But if you insist, I suppose I'll have to.'

'Not to tell lies and not to steal.'

'Oh, all right. Not to tell lies and not to steal.'

'And not to "organize" either.'

'That's enough. Anyone would think I was a criminal. You don't have to go with me. Go with the kids—you're always on their side, anyway.'

Peter stood up and ran down the garden path between the flower-beds.

Peps laughed. 'You two are always quarrelling. You can see what Peter's like now.'

'You be quiet. I like Peter much more than you, I can tell you! And without him we should never get home.'

At that moment the old woman came out of the house carrying a large bowl. She put four spoons by it and said, 'I haven't any plates. Eat it up and don't quarrel, even though there is only one bowl.'

Gisela called Peter, and immediately they were sitting happily together eating their fill.

7

For the first few days the walking was a novelty. There were all kinds of things to see; the sun shone, and everything went smoothly. But after a while, the boys became discontented.

Peter said shortly that anyone who didn't want to go or who didn't like it could stay behind. But Gisela intervened. And then she began to tell stories to make the time pass more quickly. She told whatever stories came into her head. Fairy stories and Bible stories, from the wedding at Cana and the men in the fiery furnace to Little Red Riding Hood and Hansel and Gretel. She always explained that one sort were really true and actually happened, and that the other sort were only fairy-tales.

But Peter used to say, 'That's just impossible!' even about the Bible stories.

Then Gisela stood in the middle of the road, stamped her foot, and became quite red in the face with anger.

'It *is* true, and it *did* really happen! If you're still not going to believe, later on you'll see what God will do with you! Everything in the Bible is true and really happened, but you are stupid, and you don't know because you never learnt.'

'Come on, don't let's squabble. When you get so angry you're quite a little cat.'

'And you—and you, you're, you're absolutely impossible! You always make me lose my temper, and I shan't tell any more stories if you're going to be like that.'

'Don't take any notice of him, Gisela! You go on telling us—he doesn't need to listen if he doesn't believe it,' broke in Peps, who found the story-telling very pleasant and entertaining.

But they always made it up quickly.

Sometimes, when small groups of refugees passed by, the children would join up with them. But as soon as anyone offered to take Gisela with them, Peter would immediately leave the group again. He arranged it very skilfully, so that the children either got left behind, or set off very early in the morning before the others were ready. Heini and Peps were always on their guard then, and Gisela had to promise them that she would see that Peter didn't go off with her without taking them.

They made only slow progress. The children began to look more and more bedraggled and dirty. The boys' hair had grown long round their necks and Gisela's plaits were terribly tangled. Their clothes were dusty, torn and faded. People who saw the children would shake their heads. But they didn't allow anyone to stop them. The younger boys would not be parted from Gisela, and Peter had to take them with him for better or worse, even though he would have dearly liked to get rid of them.

The days were hot and long now. At midday they usually had a long rest somewhere in the shade. To make up for this, Peter always set off very early in the morning.

Then the business of Heini's shoes began. They were marching along a dusty path at the side of a field when Heini literally lost his left shoe. He began to wail, 'How can I go any further now? Can't you do anything to mend it, with string or something?'

'String! Where are we supposed to get string here? Anyway, it wouldn't be any good. It's very warm—take the other off and walk barefoot.'

The other shoe came off more quickly than Peter had anticipated. Heini kicked out his leg violently and the remains of the shoe flew high into the air, and landed in a ditch.

'There you are. That's much better than worn-out old shoes on your feet.'

'No, it's not better! It hurts my feet. The stones stick into me!'

Heini picked his way with little, cautious steps. Peter laughed out loud.

'Just look at him, Gisela! He looks like a stork in a cabbage patch! Can't you walk barefoot, Heini?'

'You can laugh! But it hurts! You're a beast!'

'Heavens, Gisela! Whatever shall we do with him? If he carries on like this, we'll never get there.'

'I'll give him my shoes.'

'What about you?'

'I can walk barefoot. I quite like it.' Gisela sat down by the path and prepared to take off her shoes.

'No, not you! You're a girl! It would be better for Peps to give his shoes and walk barefoot.'

'*My* shoes? Do you really think I'm going to give him *my* shoes? I'm only too glad they're still lasting.'

All four of them stood, perplexed and discouraged, not knowing what to do, looking first at each other and then at Heini's bare feet.

'Oh, come on—let's leave him—he'll soon learn to walk barefoot.'

Heini let out a dreadful wail. Gisela gave Peter a look of despair, but Peter pretended not to notice.

Gisela tilted her head. 'Heini, Peps! Come on! *We'll* sit down here in the grass. I'm tired. We'll have a rest first, then something to eat, then perhaps we'll think of something.'

'I'd be glad if you'd tell me how we're going to get any further with a lame Heini,' said Peter. 'We can't just stay sitting here.'

'Mummy always used to say when you can't do anything else, you can always pray.'

'But that won't get Heini any shoes.'

'It might!'

'Do be reasonable! No shoes will come flying through the air when you pray.'

Heini and Peps had been listening in silence. Now Peps joined in.

'You don't need to believe, Peter. Let Gisela get on

with it. You're only annoyed because you don't know how to pray!'

'Neither do you!'

'Gisela, you think, don't you, because the Saviour could make wine out of water, then He can make shoes out of a stone or a piece of wood,' said Heini.

'No, that's not what I mean at all. But the Saviour will help somehow.'

Peter unwrapped the bundle. That morning a farmer's wife had given him some bread for the journey. They shared it out between them and pulled up sorrel from the hedge to eat with it.

Peter finished first and looked around to see where he could get help for Heini. Begging for shoes was out of the question. It was difficult enough to get food. When he turned to Gisela, she was sitting with her head bent and her hands folded. He was astonished. There she sat, praying, and really believed that God would help! If only He would! But shoes? That was simply impossible in the middle of the country and at a time like this.

When she looked up again, she smiled.

Peter sat down beside her on the grass.

'Have you been praying? Look, little girl, I don't know about God. Maybe He is very powerful, but it's absolutely impossible to get shoes for Heini here in the middle of nowhere, with not a soul in sight. You must see that. But we must do something. We can't just sit here and wait for Heini's shoes. We must move on. We've had an awfully long rest, and we've hardly walked any distance at all today. Think how far it is. We must go on, even without shoes. At least we must get to a village. Perhaps we could leave Heini there somewhere.'

'He just wants to get rid of me! If only I'd still got my shoes! I'll walk barefoot,' shouted Heini defiantly.

'Oh, stop your wailing!' Peter threatened the younger boy with his fist. 'Come on, Gisela, let's go. He'll have to look after himself.'

'Now then, what are you youngsters doing here?'

The children turned round, startled. A man and a young woman were coming out of the wood behind them.

'Oh,' said Gisela, and looked triumphantly at Peter.

He answered the stranger. 'We've been having a rest here.'

Gisela nodded in agreement. 'Yes, we've been waiting.'

'What for?'

Peter grinned. 'For shoes for Heini!' He pointed to the younger boy.

'Oh, you poor creatures! Wherever have you come from? Just look at you! And where are you going? Where are your parents? Or who else is there with you?'

'You mustn't ask so many questions all at once,' said the man to the sympathetic lady. 'Now, what's the matter with the shoes?'

Gisela had stood up. Standing there, dirty, weather-beaten, her hair tangled, her dress worn out, she was a sorry sight.

'We're going to Düsseldorf together. It's quite a long way.'

'To Düsseldorf? But that's impossible!'

'Just let her finish telling us, Dina'.

'Oh, yes, I know it's a long way, but we'll get there. Only Heini's shoes are worn out, and he's quite small and can't walk barefoot very well.'

'But how are you going to find the way?'

'Oh, Peter knows the way.' Gisela pointed to her protector. 'We always go in the direction in which the sun sets. We've already come quite a long way. It's just that Heini's shoes are worn out.'

'Why must you go so far?'

'Because I'm going to meet my mother there.'

'Are you all one family?'

'No, but we belong together.'

Then the woman said something to her husband which Gisela didn't hear. Peter stood on one side glowering, anxious to know what would happen.

The man nodded, and then the lady continued, turning to Gisela.

'Look, suppose you come home with us first—we live there.' She pointed in the direction of the forest. We'll give a piggy-back to the little boy without shoes. You three can walk, can't you?'

The little procession made its way through the forest.

Gisela drew level with Peter. 'Didn't I tell you? You'll see. He will help.'

'Maybe. We shall see.'

'Yes, we definitely shall see. I'm so glad. And then you'll believe as well, won't you, Peter?'

The boy was silent.

'I do so want you to believe as well. It must be because of the Saviour that the people found us.'

'We'll wait and see, Gisela.'

'Peter, why *won't* you believe?'

'I don't know. But perhaps I'll believe a little bit if Heini does get some shoes. But it will be very strange. All because you sat there in the ditch and spoke to yourself. I don't know what to think.'

'But I wasn't just speaking to myself. I was praying a proper prayer.'

'There you are, you see, that's what I don't understand. You sit there and pray, and suddenly people who are out walking, or something, pass by—is that supposed to be because of the prayer? They would have come anyway, I'm sure. It's got nothing to do with God and praying.'

'Peter, why don't you want to believe?' asked Gisela again.

'I just can't.'

'Well, I shall go on praying that you will be able to one day.'

The forest came to an end suddenly, and they found themselves standing in a field. A narrow path led up to a friendly white cottage among the fruit trees.

'I think you should first of all wash yourselves thoroughly and comb your hair. While you're doing that, I'll make a nice soup for you, and then we'll discuss things.'

Nobody could have been more delighted to have soap and a hand-towel than Gisela. She washed herself vigorously, and Peter had to keep on lifting the handle of the pump so that the clear water ran over her arms and legs.

The younger boys did not share her enthusiasm. 'We shall get dirty again straightaway afterwards,' said Peps.

They could hear the clatter of plates in the kitchen, and the young woman singing softly to herself. The children began to feel quite at home, and noticed for the first time how lonely they had been on their travels.

The gentleman called Gisela to him when she was ready, and wanted to know everything: where they came from, and how they had joined up with one another.

Peter sat down on the other end of the seat. What were these people planning to do with them?

When Gisela came to the end of her story, the man called Heini.

'And now you want to go to Düsseldorf with Gisela?'

'I don't want to really. But I don't know where there is anyone I know. Mummy, or Mrs. Ebers, or Auntie Hanna, or anyone. They all went away. And Gisela found me when I was nearly starving to death, and now I don't want to leave her by herself.'

Peter laughed scornfully. 'That's a good one. He doesn't want to leave her by herself! But it's him we're always having to worry about, because he can't walk quickly enough.'

'So I suppose you'd be quite glad to get rid of him, wouldn't you?'

'No, no! We're not going just to leave him!'

'Oh, yes, we would be glad to get rid of him. I would, anyway,' said Peter. 'It's only Gisela who always takes pity on him.'

'I see. Well, I think the soup is ready. Let's go and see.'

The children sat round the table in the friendly sparkling kitchen, and when they had lost most of their hunger they began to look around them. In the corner stood a very small table and chair, and there was a carved wooden horse on a little cupboard. Who did they belong to?

'When do you want to go on?'

'Straightaway, if only we had shoes for Heini.'

'I think it would be better if you waited till the sun wasn't quite so hot. I'll give you another blanket. You've got one already. Then you can lie down in the garden under the trees and have a rest.'

Peter didn't want to, but Gisela thought it was a lovely idea, so he gave in.

'We still haven't got the shoes,' he pointed out, when they were lying in the garden.

'Wait and see! We haven't left yet either. I think we shall get some.'

Peter was silent. He lay on his back looking up into the branches and thinking.

Why did he have to keep on thinking about what Gisela had said about God and the Saviour? Why was he all the time secretly hoping they wouldn't get the shoes? Heini needed them urgently. It was hateful and unreasonable to wish a thing like that. Was it just to prove Gisela wrong? No, he didn't want to hurt Gisela. But he didn't want anything to do with this Saviour. This God must not be proved right. But if they were helped with shoes for Heini it would look as though it was all true. It would look as though this was because of the prayer. That was just what Peter didn't want. Because then he would almost have to believe that there was something in it; that Gisela was right after all, and that this God did hear when you prayed. But he wanted to prove the opposite. Not to hurt Gisela, but to hurt God.

'I'm just being stupid,' he concluded finally to himself. 'It's all pure chance. Gisela can think it comes from God if she likes.'

They heard footsteps on the path. The young woman sat down on the grass near the children.

'Do you really believe that you will get to Düsseldorf?'

'Oh, yes. Even if it does take rather a long time.'

'And are you sure that your mother will be there?'

'Almost sure. We always lived there before. So she'll go back there and wait for me to come.'

'And what about you?' The lady turned to Peter.

'Well, I can't let her go alone.'

'Haven't you any parents?'

Peter shook his head.

'You poor boy! Will you be able to stay in Düsseldorf?'

'Of course he will! Mummy will keep him with us, especially when he's taken me all the way home.'

'What about the other two?'

'I'll go with them. I don't mind,' Peps assured her earnestly.

'But you would like to get rid of Heini?'

Peter was listening hard. This was the second time the question had been asked. Perhaps this was an opportunity to get rid of him once and for all.

'Gisela would never desert him. But as far as I'm concerned . . .'

'But, Peter!'

'Just a minute. Listen. I had a little boy once. He was just about as old as Heini. I think his clothes would fit Heini—trousers, socks and shoes.'

At this point Gisela jumped up.

'Shoes, shoes, shoes! Hooray! I just knew! Ha, ha, Peter, shoes for Heini!'

'Now then, what's all this? Why are you so pleased? Let me finish. I've been thinking. Because he can't walk very well and there's still such a long way to go, and because there isn't anyone who belongs to him in Düsseldorf, it might be better if he stayed here until we find his mother. He can sleep in my little boy's bed and wear his clothes.'

'Do you mean I could stay here?'

'Wouldn't you like to? It would be much better than all that walking.'

'I'd like it a lot, only I don't know what Gisela wants.'

'If he would like to stay, we wouldn't try to stop him,'

Peter broke in hurriedly. 'If he's going to be looked after, Gisela, and if they're going to look for his mother, it's the best possible thing for him.' And a marvellous way of getting rid of him, he added to himself. He looked anxiously at Gisela.

She was standing quite still with her hands folded, but he didn't hear a sound. Then she sighed happily, and said slowly, a way that was unusual for her: 'This is much better than I had ever thought. I'm so glad about it.'

Peter bent down to pick up the blanket and pillow, and rolled up the bundle in the usual way. He was afraid that something might cause them to change their minds, and said briskly, 'Come on, we've wasted enough time. We can be on our way now.'

'Why the sudden hurry?' laughed the lady. 'I want to give you some food for the journey.'

The man came out of the house and walked over to the group.

'Have you persuaded them?'

The lady nodded with a happy smile.

'Come on, then, Heini, we'll go and see whether the shoes fit.'

The man swung the little boy on to his shoulders, and took him into the house.

8

'CAN YOU see those spires over there?' Peter pointed into the distance where the outlines of buildings could be seen against the sky in the evening sunshine. Gisela, who had lain down on the grass at the side of the road, overcome with weariness, lifted herself a little, looked in the appropriate direction and nodded.

'That's Leipzig, Gisela. You must have heard about it in school. That's about halfway to Düsseldorf. If we carry on at the same rate . . .'

He stopped in the middle of his sentence and listened. Gisela had heard it too. Somewhere they could hear the whistle of an engine.

'A train!' they said, as if with one voice.

'A train? Are we going by train now?' Peps wanted to know.

'Stupid! Where do you think we'd get the money? For three people as well.'

'Yes,' Gisela sighed, 'it's bound to cost a lot of money. And we haven't any.'

Peter looked down at the girl lying weak and exhausted in the grass. He would have done anything for her—told lies and stolen, if it would help her to get home more quickly. He himself would follow on foot. He would get there much more quickly on his own. In the last day or two they had only managed a few miles. Peter realized only too clearly that Gisela could not walk much further. She never complained, but she was no longer her usual happy, contented, sometimes obstinate self. It was a long time since she had stamped her foot. Instead, she let Peter have his own way in everything. She didn't even stick up for Peps when Peter told him off.

'There's a barn over there. Can you walk just a little bit further, Gisela?'

The girl struggled to her feet.

'Tomorrow I'll go into the town. No one would notice me among so many people, and the war has been over a long time. You can rest in the barn while I'm away. I'll go and ask what it would cost to go by train. Then I'll see; perhaps I could even get the money for you.'

'Peter, you promised!'

'Oh, yes, I know. But this is something different. I'm not going to steal; I'll just borrow.'

'Do you know anyone who will lend you money?'

'No, but I thought—in a shop somewhere, a baker's or—anyway, be quiet, and don't interrupt! I'll remember exactly where it is, and afterwards you can send the money back from Düsseldorf.'

'No, no, Peter! I'd rather walk. Suppose something happened and we couldn't give it back? What would the people think?'

'Your mother could write and explain.'

Gisela shook her head wearily. Slowly the three children made their way across the field. The sun was like a red ball of fire on the horizon.

'Look, Gisela, there, where the sun is setting. That's west, and that's the way we must go. It's quite quick by train.'

Gisela didn't answer.

'Now you can see we've been going the right way. Always in the direction of the setting sun. We'll get to your home some day.'

The boy fell silent. When they came to the barn he stopped and looked around.

'It's by far the best thing to stay here for the night. Perhaps we could go through the town after all. Perhaps we could travel a little way by tram. That would get us a bit further.'

The children prepared places to sleep in the usual way. Peps fell asleep quickly, but Gisela tossed about restlessly.

'Can't you sleep?' asked Peter.

There was no answer. Slowly the night drew on. It was warm and the scent of ripening corn wafted across the field. Peter listened to Gisela's breathing. It wasn't usually so irregular. She didn't usually breathe so heavily.

The boy's hand groped towards her in the dark.

'Gisela!' he called quietly. There was her small face. He felt her hot breath on his outstretched hand.

Startled, he bent over her. Was she ill? How hot her forehead was! Had she buried herself too deep in the straw? Her head had slipped off the pillow. Carefully he eased it under her head again and stroked the hair out of her face. Ill? That would just about be the end! Ill! What was to become of them if Gisela couldn't walk any further? She had been growing much weaker for several days. He had noticed it all the time.

Peter felt an icy grip on his heart. He got up, walked round the barn, leaned against one of the posts, and stared up into the sky.

'God, Saviour, please help! Don't let Gisela be ill. Oh, God, don't let her die!'

He pressed his fists into his eyes.

It was all nonsense—God? Why should God bother about Gisela being ill?

Peter went back to the hay and listened.

'Gisela, Gisela, are you in pain? Are you ill, Gisela?' he asked in a half-whisper, close to her ear.

'Peter?' her voice trembled.

'Gisela, you are so hot. Is something wrong with you? Is something hurting?'

'I'm so tired, Peter.'

'Try to sleep. Gisela. Don't be ill, will you? We'll soon be home.'

Her answer was a confused murmur.

Again the boy walked restlessly up and down. Where was he to get help for Gisela? Why didn't this God take pity on her? After all, she prayed to Him every day. She thanked Him for every dry crust and every raw carrot which they found by the roadside, as if everything came from her dear God, her Saviour. But even though she believed it, he simply could not believe that a Saviour would bother about such little things. He could not, and he would not.

Why did he keep on thinking about this God? Now He was even letting the poor girl become ill, letting her die! Out in the open. Along the road. What kind of a God was that!

He threw himself into the straw next to Gisela, buried his face in his hands and finally fell asleep, exhausted by the troubles of the day.

9

GISELA had never looked so weak and pale as she did on this particular morning. She could hardly stand up. Peter, who had been lying awake for some little time, had reached a decision.

'Listen, Gisela. I'll go into town today. Perhaps I'll be able to find some work. I'll try, anyway. And when I've got enough money together, then I'll put you on a train to Düsseldorf, and follow by myself on foot.'

Wearily Gisela raised her head. 'Yes, perhaps that would work.'

'And what are we supposed to do until you've got the money? And am I supposed to go to Düsseldorf on my own with you? I'll always be thinking you're trying to shake me off, and then, what? What am I supposed to do then?' Peps complained.

'Be quiet, you!' Peter glared at him.

'Gisela, can you walk a little way? Please try. We must find somewhere for you to stay.'

'I can manage, Peter.' She got up with difficulty, but swayed and had to lean on Peps for support. He looked at her anxiously.

First of all, Peter guided them towards a farm which lay on the road which seemed to lead right into the town. Normally he would have avoided such a road at all costs. But now he was only concerned about one thing, to get Gisela some food.

An old man was just coming out of the gate as the children limped up to it. Peter, who hated nothing so much as begging, spoke to the man.

'This little girl,' he made a helpless gesture, 'it would be good if she could have a little milk.'

'Are there beggars on the road even this early in the morning?' The high-pitched voice shouting from one of the windows sounded angry. Peter flushed to the roots of his hair. He was about to reply indignantly when the man put his finger to his lips.

'Quiet, lad. There are so many coming every day. Things are bad just now—everyone is hungry. I'll fetch the little one some milk. Wait there. Round the corner is a bench she can sit on.'

They went to the side of the house, found the bench, and Gisela leaned against Peter's shoulder.

'I'm so cold, Peter.'

'Cold? In this heat? Gisela, where does it hurt? What's wrong with you? You just mustn't be ill!'

'It will be better again soon.'

Then they sat together in silence. Peps didn't dare say anything. Peter was in one of his moods. He had noticed this as soon as they got up. And Gisela was different, too, not so happy and good as usual. She looked so strange. Her eyes were big and her face seemed quite small—she must surely be ill. Peps began to feel afraid.

'The old man has forgotten us. He's probably got plenty to eat himself. He doesn't know what it's like to have to walk with an empty stomach.'

'Peter.' Gisela's voice seemed little more than a breath. Then she folded her hands.

Peter could have screamed. Everything in him cried out against praying, against this God. If the old man did come and bring food after all, then it would look . . .

At that moment he came round the corner.

'There you are, children, sshh! It took rather a long time. I've put one or two things together for you. Look, there's bacon and bread wrapped in the cloth. But drink the milk now, because I must take the jug back.'

'Gisela first!' Peter pushed Peps on one side when he jumped up and reached out for the beaker which the old man had filled with milk.

With a smile Gisela took it, drank one gulp and then put it down again.

'Dear Lord, thank You for the lovely milk.'

The kind old man looked at her and shook his head.

'Prayer? Is there still such a thing in the world? Prayer for a drop of milk!'

He wiped his eyes with the back of his hand.

Gisela did not empty the beaker, but handed it to Peps.

'But leave some for Peter.'

'Drink it up, lassie, drink it up. There's enough left in the jug for the boys.'

There was a shout from the house. The old man looked round and put his finger to his lips again.

'Sshh! My daughter's calling me. You'd better move on when you've finished drinking. All day long people come begging for corn and bread. These are terrible times, and that child can still pray.' Shaking his head, he took the empty jug back into the house.

'Peter, I shall be able to walk much further now. The milk has done me a lot of good. If only you could pray, too, everything would be much easier.'

Peter shrugged his shoulders. He picked up the bundle, after he had looked to see what the old man had wrapped in the cloth. Then he told them which way to go.

But it didn't last long. They could just see the first houses of the town ahead of them when Gisela suddenly collapsed.

'Gisela!' Peter almost shouted, he was so worried. 'Here, Peps, take the bundle. I'll carry Gisela.'

He struggled to carry her, but she became too much for him, and he had to put her on the ground again. He felt discouraged.

After a while Gisela struggled to her feet again. Supported by the two boys she managed to stagger along one step at a time. In this way they reached the shade of a park.

In spite of the fact that it was still morning, it was oppressively hot. Peter led the way to a tree and spread the blanket carefully on the grass. Gisela sank down on to it with a deep sigh, closed her eyes and lay quite still.

Peter felt the icy fingers round his heart again. Peps looked at him anxiously. He didn't dare speak, even to ask a question. When Peter looked like this it was best to keep silent. At least Peps had come to realize that much. He sat down on the grass near Gisela.

Peter didn't seem to see him. He stared with his eyes fixed on the girl lying there. Suddenly he turned on his heel and ran towards the grey dusty road which led into the town.

Peter had already caught himself praying for help. Now it happened a second time. He was furious with himself. He refused to admit that he did have a tiny, faint hope that it would perhaps be of some use. That it might be a good thing to be able to turn to this God, to Gisela's Saviour.

Fold his hands—no, he certainly wouldn't do that! He mustn't let anyone see that he was thinking such thoughts. He mustn't even move his lips. He did the opposite and pressed them firmly together, so as not to give himself away. He didn't even want to admit it to himself, let alone Peps who had been watching him so intently. Peter had been well aware of that.

He could not believe that God would help him. It was different with Gisela. She was kind and gentle. And she prayed properly, in the way that would please God, if this God really existed. Perhaps He did exist for Gisela, but not for him. Not for someone who didn't want to believe and who often said and thought hateful things. Not for someone who would have told lies and stolen, if Gisela's pleading eyes had not prevented him. Those angels Gisela said God sent were not there for him. Why, he himself was sent by God, according to Gisela!

On the other side of the road there was an illuminated sign, a blue traffic sign, saying 'Hospital.'

Hospital!

Like a bolt from the blue the thought flashed across Peter's mind. A hospital. There would be beds there, sick people were taken in and looked after! That was the answer for Gisela. That was the right kind of help.

Might this help come from God?

Had this help come because he had made a feeble attempt to pray? Had that been a prayer, that crying inside himself, 'God in heaven, help, please help!'? But then he had run away, feeling furious with himself. Hadn't God noticed that he had become angry and had even laughed at himself? Had He helped in spite of all this?

No, it was chance, all pure chance. The milk that morning, and the food on other days. It was just that people were too kind to let three homeless children starve.

People?

'Stupid nonsense,' he blurted out.

Now he must act quickly. He must get Gisela to the hospital. Somehow he must drag her there. And after that? What would happen then? If she . . .

He pushed the thought quickly out of his mind. Gisela mustn't die. Gisela must get well again. In the meantime, he would earn money. How? This was a town. He'd find something to do. In a factory, perhaps. And when Gisela was better again, perhaps by that time he would have saved enough money for her to travel home by train.

He ran back. Peps, who had watched him go anxiously, jumped up.

'You stay here with the things, understand? I'm taking Gisela to a hospital. There's one down the road. I'll get her there somehow. You're to keep watch on the blanket and pillow, and wait. It'll be the worse for you if you run away and I catch you later. Just remember that. I don't have to have you tagging along all the time.'

'Peter, don't desert Peps.'

'Gisela, can you walk a little way? Only ever such a short distance. There's a hospital over there. You're ill, and they'll look after you there. And when you're better, we'll ride home. Come on, try just once more. Then you'll be able to have a lovely bed, and you can sleep. They'll give you food as well.'

Leaning on his arm, Gisela managed to stand up again. Half carried, half dragged, he got her as far as the steps of the hospital, which shone white against the green trees.

10

It seemed like an age to Peps. Wherever had Peter got to? In a suburban park like this there was no one about at this time in the morning. Peps began to feel afraid. He got up and peered down the street. No sign of Peter.

The sun was burning down. Peps felt hungry and thirsty. There was food wrapped in the cloth. If Peter didn't come soon, he'd make a start on it. Why was he such a long time? Why didn't he come? Would he come back at all?

Then he saw him. He was slinking along the street with his head down. Peps ran back to his place quickly.

Peter came up to him, sat down on the grass by the blanket, pulled up one of the long grasses and began chewing it. He didn't say anything—just stared into the distance.

It was some time before Peps plucked up enough courage to say quietly, 'I'm hungry.'

Peter turned slowly towards the younger boy. He looked at him as if he'd only just remembered that Peps was there.

The boy looked at him timidly and with some surprise. Peter was so different. Not angry or bad-tempered, completely changed. At length he pulled his penknife out of his pocket and said, 'There's some food here.' He handed Peps the knife.

Peps' small hands couldn't hold the large loaf properly, and he nearly cut himself. Peter took the knife and bread from him, not impatiently or angrily, but as if he were about to cut a slice for Gisela. Then he carved a few slices off the bacon and put them on the bread.

While he was doing this, Peps asked gently, 'Is she, is she in bed now?'

Peter shrugged his shoulders. 'I hope so.' He stared in front of him again.

Then in a strangely unfamiliar, broken voice, he told Peps what had happened.

'They wouldn't let us in. Gisela couldn't walk any further. She was lying on the steps in front of the door. Then a nurse came up to us. She asked a lot of questions all at once. What we wanted and who we were, and whether I couldn't read. There was a notice which said no children were allowed inside. She said it wasn't a proper hospital, but a kind of home where babies are born. And they might become ill if I took a sick girl in—oh, she went on and on. And then another nurse came, and more nurses. And the one who was probably in charge took Gisela's hand and then gave the other nurses such a queer look.'

Peps sat chewing his bread. Peter fell silent and stared in front of him again. It was some time before Peps finished his bread and asked:

'And then?'

Peter returned to the present.

'Yes, and then'—he pulled up another bit of grass and chewed it and threw it away. 'Then she said to one of the nurses—I wasn't supposed to hear, but I noticed her strange look.'

Peps watched Peter. He felt suddenly afraid and his heart began to pound. It would almost have been better if Peter had scolded or got angry with him. This strange, new Peter aroused almost as much fear in him as the old one. He didn't dare ask any more questions.

After a while Peter continued of his own accord. His voice had become even more broken. It sounded as if he had a lump in his throat.

'Then, the one who was probably in charge told the other nurse to telephone for an ambulance quickly. And then she said very quietly, but I heard every word . . .'

Peter gulped several times. Peps noticed and was surprised. Peter hadn't eaten anything. What was he swallowing so hard?

'. . . if she were to die here on our doorstep . . .'

'Peter!'

He only nodded and continued slowly and hesitantly, staring into space.

'. . . there'd be a terrible row.'

Peter jumped up suddenly and began walking up and down. Peps sat quite still by the path, feeling very troubled.

Peter stopped, his hands behind his back and looked down at him.

There sat Peps, healthy and active. Why did it have to be Gisela who was ill? Why couldn't it be Peps? And if someone had to die, why Gisela?

No! No! No! She mustn't die. He would do everything she asked him, even pray. He would try really hard to pray properly, not in the way he was doing it now, with the despair in his heart making him cry, 'Help! Please help! God or Saviour, or whoever it is that can help. Please make her stay alive!'

No, not like that—that wasn't a proper prayer. If Gisela got better again, he would ask her. He wanted her to teach him. If only she would get well. If only he would be able to take her home.

The first thing he wanted to do was work. Day and night, to earn money so that she could travel by train.

He bent down and rolled up the blanket and pillow. 'Come on, Peps! Let's go and find out where the hospital is where they've taken Gisela. The children's hospital, the nurse said.'

Peps was glad that Peter wasn't trying to get rid of him. He had no idea what was going on in Peter's mind. It would have been very easy to give Peps the slip in the town. But now Peter was glad of Peps' company. Peps was like a bit of Gisela. He could talk to him about her. And even though Peps had always seemed to Peter to be little and stupid, he had nevertheless shared the long journey with them. He knew all about the happy life in the deserted farmhouse where they had met each other. Yes, Peter was extremely glad that Peps was still with him. He had reached the point where he really wanted his company.

Neither of them gave a thought to the problem of where they would get food or spend the night. They could only think about Gisela.

'I don't know which way. We'll have to ask. The nurse said we'd have to change. She thought I'd be travelling by tram!'

'We'll find it, won't we, Peter?'

He nodded down at him.

Peps trotted contentedly at Peter's side. There was so much to see here in the town that he wasn't at all bored. Meantime Peter was busy with his thoughts.

Was Gisela really so ill? Could a person be healthy one moment and nearly dead the next? It wasn't very likely. With old people, perhaps, but he had never heard of it with children. They got measles, but they were soon better again. The nurse had probably only said this so that the ambulance would come more quickly. She was probably just sorry for Gisela.

Then Peter suddenly caught sight of a notice: 'Distribution of Ration Cards'. It was written in huge letters.

He would have to find out about that. Ration cards—he had forgotten they still existed. He began to read. Hmm. That would be a problem. The difficulties were beginning straightaway. If he told a few cunning lies he might be able to get hold of some ration cards, but he mustn't tell lies. And he didn't want to, either. He had promised Gisela. Suppose she asked him one day. That would be awful.

So bread could only be bought with coupons. Things were probably different here in the town from the country, where the farmers had corn in their fields and in their barns.

But how were they to get bread?

It was going to be even more difficult than he'd imagined. And to add to all this there was Peps, who was everlastingly hungry. But he couldn't desert him.

At least Gisela wouldn't need coupons in hospital. They couldn't let her starve just because she had no coupons. They wouldn't do that.

If only he could do what Gisela did, just pray, carry on walking, knock on someone's door, and be given food. But that only happened because the farmers always had food. He would have to try it here. If only he knew what to say when he prayed. He had always left it to Gisela before.

It had never occurred to him that he might need it some time, or that he would even want to try.

'Peps, do you think you could pray?'

'What?' Peps's eyes bulged and he stared at Peter.

'Don't stare so stupidly at me! You've been with Gisela all the time like I have. You know that she always prayed about everything. That time about Heini's shoes—it was really odd the way Heini got everything he needed from those people afterwards. Do you think it was because of Gisela's prayer?'

'Could be, perhaps. I don't really know.' Peps didn't want to give a definite answer. He didn't want to annoy Peter, and he wasn't sure which answer he wanted.

'What did she always pray when we were hungry, or when we didn't have anywhere to go when it rained, and things like that?'

'Well, she just used to behave as if this Jesus was sitting next to her or walking by her side. She used to put her hands together and just speak to Him. It always used to surprise me as well. She seemed to know Him very well, and that's just it! We don't know Him like that at all. And you can't just speak to someone you don't know, or ask for things. Do you know what I mean?'

Peter nodded. The kid wasn't as stupid as he sometimes looked.

'You could have paid a bit more attention though, Peps.'

'To the praying, d'you mean? Oh, Gisela was used to doing it and she was much better at it. I tried it once or twice, but it never worked for me.'

'There you are, you see!'

'What do you mean, "you see"?'

'Well, it probably won't work for me either! That's why I don't want to start it.'

'What are we supposed to be praying for anyway?'

Peter became impatient. 'As if there aren't enough things! First, that Gisela will get well, and then . . . oh, what's the use! It won't work, at least not for me.'

'Can't we go to Gisela and ask her?'

'She's too ill now, but later perhaps. *You* can ask her about it.'

It was already four o'clock by the time Peter and Peps reached the yellow building which was the hospital. The man in the porter's lodge eyed them suspiciously.

'We'd better not go in now.' Peter suddenly remembered what they looked like. 'He'll only chase us off. We look so dirty. We might be able to get a wash somewhere. Anyway, *I'm* hungry now as well. We'll see whether there's a place near here where we can hide. There won't be any barns or useful places like that, and if we ask at people's houses they'll only look at us and decide we're too dirty. We might be able to find a place on a bomb-site where we can hide for the time being.'

They sat down on the remains of a wall in a side street and shared the bread and bacon. Peps was amazed that he was being treated so well. In the past Peter's one concern had been that Gisela should have enough to eat. That he now gave Peps the bigger share both astonished and pleased the younger boy.

When they had finished, Peter began exploring the ruins until he found a place which still had some sort of a roof over it. This would serve as cover for the time being.

11

THERE WAS a chart hanging at the end of Gisela's bed, but the only thing that was filled in, in the bottom right-hand corner, was the date of her admission: 15.7.45.

The lady doctor looked inquiringly at the nurse and pointed to the chart.

'The child was brought in unconscious. All we heard from the women's hospital was that she collapsed outside the door there. There was a boy with her. They didn't find out her name, or where she had come from, or anything about the boy.'

'Sshh! She's saying something.' The doctor bent down over the child.

Gisela was talking incoherently in her fever.

The doctor listened for a while, then stood up again and shook her head.

'She keeps on talking about someone called Peter. I can't understand anything else.'

The nurse supported the young patient while the doctor sounded her chest and back. Then she sighed and looked thoughtfully at the thin little face. Her sun-burnt cheeks were bright with fever.

The nurse made a note of the doctor's instructions, drew the curtains round the bed again and went out.

For a while all was quiet in the ward. Then the whispering began.

'I say, Annegret, can you see the new arrival?'

Annegret, whose bed was next to Gisela's, reached over, pulled the curtain a little to one side and looked in.

'She's asleep—at least, her eyes are closed. Sshh! She's

saying something. Can't understand properly. She keeps moving her head from side to side.'

'What does she look like?'

'I'll go and find out.' That was Hannelore.

'I say, what if the nurse comes and you're out of bed?'

'Yes, your stomach will start to hurt again.'

Hannelore was already running across the ward in her bare feet. She bent over the restless little patient and listened breathlessly.

'Peter, just look at all the flowers! Oh, don't go into the house again. Peter, Peter!'

Hannelore came out from behind the screen looking pale and frightened. 'I think we ought to call the nurse. Listen! She's talking quite loudly now.'

The children sat in their beds listening to Gisela's voice, which grew louder and more troubled.

'It's so hot, Peter, and I'm so thirsty. Dear Saviour, please send Heini some shoes. Why are you running so fast, Peter?'

'I'll call the nurse.'

Then the ward orderly came with the tray.

'Aunt Sophie, listen! The new girl is talking ever so loudly in her sleep.'

'Mummy, we must take Peter with us. He showed me the way. We've come ever so far.'

The nurse came and listened.

That wouldn't do at all. The child was disturbing the whole ward. They would have to put her in the little room across the corridor.

Gisela knew nothing of what was going on around her. In her delirium she put her arms round the neck of the nurse who was transferring her.

'Mummy, Heini doesn't like beans. The fire went out because we were playing in the garden. It was so lovely in the sunshine.'

'Quiet, little one. Just go to sleep,' whispered the nurse soothingly, and gently laid the child on the pillow.

'Yes, Mummy, I need to sleep. I'm so tired.'

Then suddenly she sat bolt upright again.

'Peter! You're not to box Peps' ears. Please don't do it! He's tired from the walking as well. Is there still a long way to go? Look, there's a train. Peter, come on, let's go on the train.'

When the doctor was making her evening round she stood in silence for a while by Gisela's bed.

'If only we had some idea where the child has come from! Where are her parents? Are they still alive? Perhaps they're looking for the child, fearing the worst and completely unable to find out what has happened to her.'

The nurse nodded. 'I'm going to give her an injection; otherwise we shan't get any peace all night. The injection won't do more than quieten her down.'

Gisela didn't even flinch when the fine needle entered her thin leg. Her confused chatter continued for a little while, then it became an unintelligible murmur, and then it stopped altogether. In the middle of the night the night sister looked into the little room. Gisela was lying so still that the nurse felt for her hand quickly, almost fearing the worst. The girl's heart was still beating, but she could only just feel the pulse, it was so faint. The sister looked down at the thin face and laid the hand gently back on the blanket.

12

PETER WOKE up feeling chilly. He sat up and looked round. Gisela?

But that was yesterday. Yesterday? Yesterday at this time they had been sitting side by side in a barn. It seemed ages ago.

Peter ran his fingers through his untidy hair.

Peps was still fast asleep, wrapped in Gisela's blanket and with his head on Gisela's pillow.

Peter felt comforted to think that at least Gisela was in a proper bed now.

He wondered how she was. Whether she had slept well. Now she would probably be able to have a proper wash as well. She wouldn't need to pray that God would send them food any more. It would be brought to her bed for her now.

He wondered how long the illness would last. It couldn't be as bad as all that.

Anyway, his main job now was to see that he came by some money as quickly as possible.

But how was he to begin?

At Easter he was supposed to have started an apprenticeship. It had all been arranged. The factories were in great need of boys who were just leaving school.

But what could he do now? He had often heard farmers say that they didn't need any help. So many people would ask for work, just to get food.

Peter began to climb over the rubble. First of all he must find a place where they could stay, he and Peps. And above all Gisela, when she came out of hospital.

The sunshine was slanted on the broken wall. The

sparrows were twittering and chasing one another. What on earth they found to eat here was a complete mystery!

They reminded him of a story Gisela used to tell sometimes. It was something out of the Bible. Something about God caring even for the birds. Peter could almost hear her voice.

'There you are, Peter. If He takes care of the little birds, then He won't forget us.' And Peps had said, 'We're much bigger than the birds. He'll see us much sooner.'

And then Gisela had told them more about what was in the Bible. It had been quite pleasant to listen to her, even though it couldn't possibly all be true.

No, it couldn't be true.

But why not? Sometimes it had really seemed as if Gisela only needed to put her hands together, and help was already on the way. Gisela never seemed to think that there was anything strange about it. She just said, 'Do you still not believe that the Saviour is with us all the time?' Then she had looked at him out of the corner of her eye with her head on one side.

'Gisela,' he murmured.

The same rays of the sun which were shining into the little room at the children's hospital shone now on a half-hidden window-pane down among the ruins. Suddenly Peter became aware of the glass.

He jumped up. A window? Here amongst all the rubble, amongst all the depressing destruction?

And now he found something that he had never expected to find there.

He found a tiny house, completely undamaged. It could have been an out-house. There was a pile of rubble as high as the door-handle on the outside, but the room was completely intact. The window still had three unbroken panes.

Peter laughed to himself. Deep down in his heart he began to think that perhaps Gisela was right. after all, that God would look after them, all three of them. He must find some kind of shelter for Gisela's sake. But even he and Peps couldn't go on sleeping amongst the ruins indefinitely.

He began energetically clearing away the stones from the door. Then he heard Peps shouting.

He climbed back angrily and called to him not to shout so loudly.

'I thought you'd gone away for good. I was scared.'

'Coward! Come and help me. I've found a home for us.'

It was hard work clearing the door. Beads of perspiration stood out on Peter's face. In his enthusiasm he forgot his hunger and thirst, but Peps soon reminded him.

'Hungry! You're always hungry! Where do you think we're going to get food here in the town? There aren't any convenient farmers to give us bread and bacon. Here all the people have to have ration cards. I saw a notice about it yesterday.'

Peps stood looking disconcerted. 'What are we going to do now then? We can't just starve. What's the use of the house if we haven't got anything to eat?'

'I don't know yet what we're going to do for food. You can see if you can beg some somewhere. I'm going to find work. I don't know where, but somewhere. And I'm going to keep the money for the train fare, so that Gisela can ride home.'

'How much does it cost, then?'

Peter sat down, cupped his chin in his hand and thought. Yes, what did it cost? How far was Düsseldorf? He would have to go to the station and ask.

'Look,' he turned to Peps, 'you go off and see what you can get to eat. Don't go too far, in case you can't find the way back. I'll go on working here for a bit. When I've got the door open, I'll go to the station and ask. Then I'll come back here, understand?'

'What if you don't come back?'

Peter looked angry. 'If I say I'm coming, then I'll come! But I'm not going searching for you. You must find your own way back here. You're not little and stupid any more. Afterwards I must find out where we can have a wash and tidy ourselves up a bit. Then I'll go to the hospital and ask how Gisela is. They'll have to tell me in the end.'

Peps moped around for a while. There was nobody living round here for him to beg from. But Peter didn't pay any attention to him. He was already seeing some reward for his labours and he worked feverishly to get the door free.

It wasn't locked, but the catch had rusted badly. Peter hit it with a stone. Then he found himself standing in the low room.

A zinc tub was still hanging on the wall. Peter's eyes lit up. Gisela would be delighted to see that. She would be able to have a bath whenever she wanted it. She had always seized every opportunity to have a wash. The tap didn't work, of course, but he'd find water somewhere, even if he had to carry it some distance. He would make sure that Gisela always had fresh water.

'Are you coming with me now?' Peps asked shyly.

'Where to?'

'To get food.'

'I told you—you'll have to go on your own, and see that you don't tell a soul about this house, understand?'

Peter looked so angry and had such a threatening expression on his face that Peps nodded, trembling.

Then Peter discovered a broom behind all the rubbish. Immediately he began to sweep out one corner of the room very carefully. Then he stood back and surveyed the room, and ran out and fetched the blanket and pillow which Peps had left in the place where they had slept.

'Gisela can sleep here. Perhaps we'll be able to get some straw so that it won't be too hard for her.'

'Can I have a bit of straw too?'

'We'll have to see. Gisela comes first. She'll be used to a soft bed when she comes out, and if I haven't managed to save enough money, she might have to stay here for a while. Now go and get yourself something to eat. I can't.

I haven't got time. I must first of all go to the station, and then look for work.'

But Peps waited until Peter set off.

They went past the hospital again. Peter stopped. His heart began to beat faster. Gisela was lying behind one of those windows? Was she still asleep? Or had she woken up already? Had she been given something to eat this morning? How was she?

'Now then, what are you hanging around here for?' said a harsh voice behind them.

Peter turned round. A grey-haired, severe-looking man was standing behind them.

'I . . .' He remembered just in time that he mustn't tell a lie.

'I suppose you're one of the young urchins who are making this district unsafe?'

Peter shook his head. Making the district unsafe? That certainly didn't apply to him.

'I only wanted to find out how Gisela is.' He jerked his head in the direction of the hospital.

'Gisela? Who's Gisela?'

'She went into the hospital yesterday. She was sent here from another hospital where babies are born.'

'Aha! The little girl! So her name's Gisela. Come with me.'

Peps trotted in behind Peter.

The night porter greeted his colleague with surprise when he brought the two boys in. When he heard that they knew something about the little girl, he was immediately friendly.

Peter strained his ears to listen as the two men whispered together.

From what he could gather, Gisela was very ill and would probably soon die; she might even have died already. But no, that was not possible. The people in the hospital wanted to know her name and who her parents were. She had kept on calling for someone called Peter.

'That's me! She can only mean me! Let me go to her—you must let me go to her!'

'Steady on, lad, steady on. Of course you can go to her. The ward sister has already telephoned to say that you are to go up. So the little girl is called Gisela. Is she your sister?'

Peter shook his head.

'No. But you know what her name is and where she comes from?'

'Yes, from Düsseldorf.'

'What? Is that where you've come from?'

'Peter, shall we get something to eat here?' asked Peps in the background.

'This is a funny state of affairs. Sit down here.'

After exchanging a few routine remarks with his colleague, the night porter said good-bye and went.

Peter gritted his teeth. His heart was beating so fast he thought it would burst. Gisela, Gisela! If she was so ill, perhaps . . . No, he mustn't think about it. He mustn't think of anything so dreadful.

'Dear God, please hear me just this once when I pray. Don't let Gisela die, dear God!' As if through a haze Peter saw that Peps was holding a piece of bread and that he was being offered a piece himself. He shook his head.

'Come on, take it,' said a voice. He didn't know who it belonged to. A woman in a white overall was standing in front of him.

'Gisela,' he said in a flat tone.

'She's very ill, your little sister.'

He shook his head. The porter said something.

'I see; she isn't your sister. But you must be very fond of her. Well, I ought not to take you into the house looking as dirty as that, but in this case . . .'

He followed the woman with trembling steps. Across a courtyard, up some stairs, along long corridors. He didn't notice people staring at him, or see anyone who passed by. His only concern was to get to Gisela.

There she lay, in a white bed. Pale, thin, strangely

altered. He just stood, not daring to ask whether she was still alive. He couldn't tell whether she was breathing or not.

'Is the little girl's name Gisela?' asked someone.

He nodded.

'Gisela what? What else do you know about her?'

He gave the information without taking his eyes off her. He spoke jerkily and hesitantly.

'Fehling, from Düsseldorf. She and her mother were evacuated to a place the other side of Breslau.'

'How did you get there?'

'Walked.'

'All the way?'

'Yes, all the way.'

'Just you children?'

'Yes, the three of us. There were four of us to start with.'

'Where is the fourth?'

'Some people we met on the way looked after him.'

Suddenly he jerked himself round, looked at the sister and the doctor, and almost shouted in fear and despair, 'Is she still alive? Is she still alive?'

The sister put her hand over his mouth. 'Not so loud, not so loud! Yes, she is still alive, but you mustn't shout like that. There are a lot of very sick people in the building. And you mustn't frighten the little girl either.'

Peter covered his face with his hands. He felt a choking feeling in his throat. She was still alive, but for how long?

13

In the end Peter accepted the bread which he had been offered. He had no idea how he got into the street again. It took him some time to collect his thoughts and come to a decision. What else could he do but ask God for help? No human being could keep Gisela alive.

He ran down the street, hardly realizing that he was praying.

'Dear God, I will never steal or tell lies in my whole life again if only Gisela stays alive. Dear God, let her get better, so that I can take her home.'

Ought he to be speaking to the Saviour? Or were they the same? If only he knew. Gisela had often told him about it, but usually he hadn't been really listening. Peps had sometimes asked questions. Perhaps he knew something about it.

If only there was someone he could ask.

Peter ran across the big square. There were enormous heaps of rubble everywhere. Then he caught sight of a signpost—'Railway Station.' That was where he wanted to go. It was still just possible that God *would* help. And in case He did, Peter wanted to know the cost of the fare to Düsseldorf.

People laden with bundles, boxes and cases were thronging through the station entrance. Peter went into the main hall and looked around. There was a long queue of people in front of a ticket office. Then he spotted a man in a blue jacket wearing an arm-band. He was almost certainly a railway official and would be able to give him information.

Peter had to put up with the look of astonishment

which his inquiry produced. It was a look which examined him from head to foot in one glance.

'So you want to get to Düsseldorf, young man? But you can't go there just like that any more.'

'Not even if I had the money?'

'Not even then. New regulations are just coming out. You can't even travel to the frontier. You must get a passport first.'

'But supposing I live in Düsseldorf?'

'Then you ought to have stayed there, my lad.'

After the man had said this, he turned and left Peter standing there. By this time three or four other passengers were waiting with questions.

Peter stood there stunned. This was something completely new. Couldn't they really travel to Düsseldorf? Frontier? What kind of a frontier? Passport?

He stood feeling quite forlorn in the crowd of people thronging the hall. What was to become of them now? If Gisela couldn't go home, it might be better after all if . . . No, no, he mustn't think like that.

'Dear God!'

There I go, praying again, he thought, feeling ashamed of himself. If only it helped. Oh, if only it would help.

'Are you interested in earning yourself a bit of pocket money?'

Peter was startled. A well-dressed man had spoken to him.

'Yes, I am,' he said eagerly.

'Look, here's a ticket. Take it to the left-luggage office over there, do you see? Here's some money. You can keep the change. When you get the parcel, bring it to me. I'll show you where I'll be waiting.'

He led the way and pointed to an advertisement hoarding.

'I'll be waiting over there. Understand? And don't try any tricks with the parcel.'

Peter flushed crimson. He was about to give an indignant answer and say, '*I* don't steal!' but the man was already walking across the road, and didn't seem to be paying any more attention to him.

He obtained the parcel in question without difficulty and carried it across the hall.

'Well done! Give it here!' A stranger made as if to grab the parcel.

'What do you want? This parcel's got to be taken somewhere.'

'Yes, yes, I know. We're together, the man who gave you the ticket and the money, and me.'

'Anyone can say that! Let go the parcel or I shall shout for help.'

'Now, now, don't get so het up! We can use you. You're not as stupid as you look. We'll go together.'

Peter, full of mistrust, saw that the stranger was following him.

'Here, you boy! We often have work for a lad who's got his wits about him. We could try you. You could earn yourself quite a bit.'

'More than in a factory?'

'Factory, what factory?'

'Any factory. I wanted to work in a factory.'

'That's a good one! In a factory! Where have you been that you don't know that there isn't a factory operating—or very few anyway?'

Peter explained very briefly. The men weren't really interested in what he had to say. It was sufficient for them that he was prepared to run errands for them.

'Would you rather have money, or food?' asked the man who had spoken to him first.

That was a problem. At this particular moment Peter would have been extremely glad of something to eat. He said as much, but added that later he planned to obtain coupons, and then he would rather have the money. Then he would be able to buy bread for himself.

The real meaning of what he was learning now didn't dawn on him at first. But one thing did impress itself upon him—he couldn't just simply stay in the town.

He would have to have a residence permit, and only those who had lived there before could get one, and not even them sometimes. Bread coupons? No, he wouldn't be able to get them as easily as he'd thought, either. The men had said as much. He began to understand that it would be better for him not to bother about any of this. If he did everything they asked him to do, he wouldn't need ration cards or police permits. The best thing he could do would be to go with them and have something to eat first.

They spoke to one another in a foreign language, laughed, and clapped him on the shoulder.

'Don't worry, lad! Keep your chin up! You're a clever fellow. To get from Breslau here on foot without getting caught! That's the way to do it. Never get caught! It's a bit different here in the town, but you'll soon learn. You'll soon find out what's what.'

Well, at first he had no idea what was what. They walked together through the crowded streets, then up a narrow alley, and through a dark hall, until they came to a little door.

One of the men listened hard for a moment, then pulled a key out of his pocket and opened the door.

Peter stood still in surprise.

A smell of frying prickled his nostrils. Even the two men sniffed in anticipation.

'She's done us proud again.'

Peter found out at once who the 'she' was. A door opened and a female figure rolled in; this was the only word Peter could think of to describe the way she moved.

The woman was so fat and shapeless that to look at her you would think she was moving on unsteady wheels. Her wide skirt reached to the ground and even covered her feet. It was so strange, even comical, to see her rolling along the hall that Peter almost laughed out loud.

'Who's that you've got with you?' she asked in a squeaky voice, which sounded very strange, coming as it did from such a massive figure.

'This is our new express messenger, Dorette. He has already passed his first test in alertness and aptitude. Come on, now give us something to eat.'

Peter was pushed into a room which was very comfortably furnished. Dorette, rolling energetically to and fro brought another plate, knife and fork, and for a while Peter forgot all his troubles. It was such a long time since he had had a meal like this that for the time being all he could think of was how marvellous it tasted, and how good it was to be able to eat his fill sitting at a table.

Even now nobody seemed to want to know much about him when Peter volunteered information. And since he was only prepared to say as little as possible anyway, he sat largely in silence.

He finished his meal much more quickly than the others, who sat chatting with Dorette in a foreign language. Sometimes they looked at him, and finally the woman said, 'You really do look bedraggled. We'll have a look presently and see whether one of the jackets in the cupboard will fit you. There might be a pair of trousers too. What are your shoes like?

After a while she took him into a bathroom. He was amazed to find such luxury in the flat. He would never have guessed that so much lay behind the little door. He didn't find out until much later that the door which they used was a back entrance. The front entrance was a wide glass door which opened on to a modern staircase.

When he left the flat through the little door it was quite a different Peter from the one who had entered an hour or two before, ragged and hungry. He was wearing a decent jacket, and felt fuller inside than he had felt for a long time. One of the men had pressed a note into his hand.

'Go and get your hair cut, and come back tomorrow morning at ten o'clock. And remember, don't tell a soul! Understand?'

Peter only nodded. He felt that there was something not quite right about all this, but what did it matter to him? He was earning money, and that was all he wanted.

14

IF HE hadn't been so worried about Gisela, Peter could almost have wished for nothing more. For his message-carrying he not only received regular payment but also a good and ample midday meal. If he was released from his duties early in the afternoon, Dorette would give him a thick sandwich to take with him so that he didn't go hungry.

Peter went to the hospital every day. The porter always let him pass, because the ward sister had said Peter should be allowed to go in as often as he liked while Gisela was still alive. So Peter would run across the yard, up the stairs, and along the long corridor, and then stand beside the patient's bed. Almost every day it was the same: Gisela lay pale and motionless on her pillow. Peter could hardly hear her breathing.

Once he came in the evening. He had had to run errands all day long, right from early morning, and he hadn't had time during the day. The nurses were all busy and nobody paid attention to him. He ran up to Gisela's room as usual and found her delirious. This was something completely new for him. Frightened, he listened to her confused talking.

'It's so hot, Peter; come into the forest. I should like to sleep. Just look at all the flowers. I'll take some with me for Mummy. No, no, you mustn't go into the house again!'

The boy felt his heart begin to pound. He bent down over the feverish girl and whispered in her ear, 'Gisela, wake up. We're going home. I've already earned a lot of money. You'll be able to go by train.'

Her thin hands moved across the blanket towards him.

'Peter?'

'Yes, I'm here, Gisela. I shan't desert you.'

He racked his brains to think of something to say which would make her happy. But he knew really, he knew only too well. And even though it was so difficult for him to speak about it, he pulled himself together and said,

'Gisela, I pray every day that you will get better.'

'Peter?' The question came faintly from her pale lips.

Was she smiling? It almost seemed to Peter that she was.

But now she chattered on. 'Chocolate, oh, Mummy, I haven't had any for ages. Give me a piece, please, please!'

Then the nurse came.

'You must go now. Why do you come so late in the evening? The doctor will be making his rounds soon. Don't let him catch you, otherwise you won't be allowed to come here so often.'

Peter looked at Gisela once more, then disappeared.

With head down, he slipped along to his home in the old wash-kitchen. Peps wasn't there yet. Peter was glad. He wanted to think, and didn't feel in the mood to listen to the younger boy's chatter about the experiences of the day.

He sat down on the broken wall and turned these things over in his mind. What about his prayer? Had it been any use? Was it helping? Would Gisela stay alive? He pulled a few notes from his pocket, looked about him carefully, and then removed a loose stone from the wall. It revealed a small cavity. Inside were all his savings. He had saved very hard. When Gisela was well again they would travel together as far as it was possible for them to go. He'd get the tickets somehow. Everything was so difficult at the moment. He would have to travel with her so that they could cross the frontier together. It couldn't be as difficult as all that to get across this frontier. After all, it was just as much Germany on the other side as it was on this side. And nobody would say anything, even supposing they met anyone who could stop them.

Peter had no real idea how things would work out. All he knew was that he would do everything in his power to take Gisela home. The thought that her mother might not be in Düsseldorf at all never occurred to him. Peter stuffed the notes into the cavity, replaced the stone carefully, and scattered some sand into the cracks. Peps knew nothing about all the treasure he'd saved up. Peter smiled to himself when he thought how quickly his small fortune had grown. He had very quickly learnt what to do. He just walked along, and if he met someone who looked as though he could pay, he would say very quietly, 'Cigarettes, would you like some cigarettes?' The interested party would then murmur quietly, 'Brand?' If he had Amis, he got more than for German brands. Or he might just murmur straightaway, 'Amis, Amis, two for a mark.' It was a pity he only ever had two or three to sell at a time.

When he had delivered the parcels and had eaten dinner or supper with the others, they sometimes offered him a cigarette. He always took one, but never smoked it. Then the two men would laugh. Peter only knew their Christian names, Fritz and Alfred. And they had only asked him his first name.

'Peter,' they had said to him on the third day of his new employment, 'suppose someone were to ask you what was in the parcels. What would you say?'

'I don't know. But if anyone came up to me and wanted anything, I'd be off like a shot.'

'Fine, Peter. Obviously you've already realized what's what. But let's say a policeman came and wanted to take you to the police station.'

'There isn't much of a police force round here.'

'Well, things do happen now and again, and a man

would be much stronger than you. Supposing they ask you where you're taking the parcels?'

'If I don't feel like telling them, they'll have to drag it out of me.'

'Suppose they catch you red-handed. It would be better if you'd thought beforehand how to wriggle out of the situation without giving us away.'

Peter had looked at the two men suspiciously.

'Is the stuff in the parcels pinched?'

'That's a good one! No, it's not pinched, although we ought to box your ears for suggesting it. But we've got thick skins. It doesn't concern you where the things come from. And in any case, it's better that you shouldn't know anything. But you must never say where you are taking the parcels. How you get them there doesn't matter in the slightest. But take care not to get caught. You would be in serious trouble.'

There was something not quite right about this parcel business, but what did it matter to him? He wasn't telling lies anyway, and he hadn't stolen anything either.

He didn't feel completely happy about the affair, but it had so many advantages. Soon he would have enough money to pay both his and Gisela's fare.

And Peps? What was he going to do about Peps? Would it work again, if Gisela prayed? He was kept busy enough, praying that Gisela would get better. He was doing everything for Gisela's sake—carrying parcels, saving money, not stealing and not telling lies. Actually, stealing would have been much simpler and easier than delivering the parcels. It was a dangerous job, apart from anything else. So far everything had gone smoothly. If a policeman came into view—there were often quite a number of them at the station—he would make a detour to escape any possible danger. When he was selling the few cigarettes he had managed to save up, he might also come up against the wrong person. All the same, the risk involved appealed to his adventurous spirit. Without the prickly feeling of danger he would soon have become bored by the errands.

But he knew that there was something wrong somewhere. And the fact that he felt this was Gisela's fault as well. What would she say about it? She mustn't know what was going on.

Peter talked himself vigorously into believing that he was perfectly innocent, even if there was something fishy about the business. He fetched and carried parcels. He didn't know what was in them. But then came the prick of conscience again. 'Don't you know, really?' No, he pretended to himself that he didn't know. He could imagine what was in them, but to imagine something and to know something were two entirely different things. What did it matter to him, anyway? He didn't want to know anything about it. Angry at the struggle going on in his mind, he stood up and looked for something to vent his anger on.

At that moment Peps appeared.

'Where do you think you've been? It's getting dark. What have you been doing all day?'

Peps looked cross. He had had a bad day and was hungry.

'Well, you couldn't care less about me any more—so I have to look after myself and get food from other people. We didn't get much today. And then that big fat chap ate everything himself and we had to stand by and watch him!'

'Why do you always go around with others? It's your fault if they eat your share. You're likely to get caught if you always go round in a gang. It's much better on your own. I hope to goodness I'll get rid of you soon!'

'And I wish that Gisela would come back. She would see that I got my share. You eat everything yourself as well.'

'If you don't shut up you'll get a box on the ears. That'll make you stop feeling sorry for yourself.'

Peter was wearing his angry expression, and Peps decided he had better keep silent.

15

GISELA OPENED her eyes, blinked a little and tried to sit up, but she sank back again immediately.

She closed her eyes again and tried to remember.

What kind of a room was this? Where was she? What had she been dreaming? She couldn't think straight at all. She gave a deep sigh.

The door clicked. Gisela wondered who was coming. She opened her eyes again and looked in astonishment at the nurse.

'Has our little stranger woken up? The doctor will be very pleased.'

Gisela smiled. 'The doctor?'

'Yes, the doctor, Gisela. We have been looking after you for a long time, and have been very worried about you. We're all very pleased that you're better now.'

Gisela was about to ask something else, but her eyes had already closed again.

At midday Peter came. As usual he ran up to the little room without speaking to anyone. The nurse saw him and ran after him.

'Peter, stop! There's something I must tell you.'

The boy stopped in his tracks. His legs felt strangely weak. His heart began to pound. He looked at the nurse in horror.

'No, you needn't look so scared. Gisela is much better. I almost believe that she'll be well again soon. She is conscious but still very weak. You mustn't get her excited. Just look in quickly. If she's asleep, don't wake her. Come along, perhaps I'd better go with you.'

Peter would much rather have gone alone, but the nurse already had her hand on the door handle.

'Quietly, and don't excite her. Do you understand?'

How he could possibly get Gisela excited was not at all clear to Peter. He tiptoed into the room.

'Quiet, she's asleep.'

But Gisela wasn't asleep. She looked up and saw Peter.

The sight of him must have brought all the memories flooding back. Her eyes widened as she looked at Peter, and suddenly she burst into tears.

Peter rushed over to her—the nurse couldn't stop him. 'Gisela, don't cry! Don't cry! You'll soon be better now. And then we'll travel home to your mother. I've already saved up a lot of money.'

'That's enough! You'll get her too excited.' The nurse seized the boy firmly.

To Gisela she said, 'Peter must go now. He can come again tomorrow. The doctor will be very cross if you make yourself worse again.'

'Peter,' gasped Gisela, and the tears streamed down her face.

Suddenly she remembered everything vividly. The trek. The long journey in the winter through the ice and snow. Her mother not being there. The deserted house where she found Peter, and Heini and Peps. The journey, the long journey. And Peter, always Peter. And they were going home. Oh, how she wanted to go home!

Her brain refused to think any more. Sleep overtook her—gentle, refreshing, healing sleep.

The next day Peter came as usual to the hospital. When he went into the little room he found it empty. But before he could start to worry, the nurse was there, and said, 'Well, my boy, your Gisela is in the ward with the other children now. So you won't be able to come at any time of the day any more. You'll have to keep to normal visiting hours, like all the other people.'

'But yesterday you told Gisela that I could come again today.'

'So I did. I told her that to calm her down.'

'Well, that's all right then. I'll go and see her again now.'

'But I've just told you, you must keep to visiting hours.'

'Well, then, you told a lie yesterday.'

'Whatever are you thinking of, you cheeky boy!'

'It's true. Afterwards Gisela will think that I didn't keep my word.'

'Just be off with you. Otherwise I shan't let you in again at all.'

Tears of anger welled up in Peter's eyes. He stood facing the nurse, feeling completely helpless. He didn't even know where Gisela was. Perhaps she had died after all, and they didn't want to tell him.

'She's dead! Yes, that's it: she's dead and you don't want to tell me,' he said between clenched teeth.

Then they heard footsteps along the corridor. The young lady doctor looked at Peter and noticed his troubled, unsmiling face.

'Now then, what's all this? Our little patient is much better. We don't need to pull such a long face.'

'I've just explained to him that Gisela is in the ward with the other children now, and that he must keep to visiting hours.'

'The nurse is quite right, my boy—but we'll allow him just one more visit, shall we, nurse? In future he will come at the proper visiting time. Now just say Hallo quickly, and then disappear.'

Today Gisela was not crying. She smiled at Peter and was even able to talk a little.

'You'll never believe it, Peter, but I dreamt that you said, "I pray every day that you'll get better." '

'Well, so I do.'

'Peter—oh, dear Peter!'

The boy took her small transparent hand in his rough one, held it for a moment, and then laid it carefully back on the blanket, as if he were afraid it might break.

A lump came into his throat. He couldn't manage to say anything else. He nodded to Gisela and turned towards the door.

Outside he considered: today was Thursday. He would

have to wait until Sunday before he could see Gisela again.

Sunday. Between now and then he must get hold of some chocolate. If it was possible to buy cigarettes, it must be possible to buy chocolate too. He would ask someone. Dorette would know perhaps.

Dorette didn't know. She told him to ask Fritz and Alfred. They would be able to tell him. But chocolate was expensive. A block might cost as much as twenty marks.

Peter's head swam. Twenty marks? Could he spare that much from his fare-money?

He wondered whether he might be able to buy just a piece. It didn't have to be a whole block. Three or four squares would be enough.

Fritz laughed when he heard what Peter wanted. Yes, it was possible to get chocolate. Small blocks cost seven marks.

'I've got a parcel here that has to go to Lessing Street. You can ask about chocolate there. They've usually got some. If you say it's for me, you'll get it for five marks.'

Peter reddened. So it was a question of telling lies again if he wanted to get it cheaper. He bit his bottom lip and took the parcel. On the way he fought the battle inside him which always occurred in this sort of situation. Two marks. That was a lot of money for him. It had to be earned first. And here it was earned so quickly if he just told one small fib. That couldn't exactly be called telling lies. He wondered whether Gisela would agree. Gisela? If only there was just Gisela. But for some time now there had been someone else behind all his thinking. This Saviour and God. He hadn't only promised Gisela not to tell lies or steal, he had promised God. But everyone made rash promises when they were in need and despair. Would God be as particular as that? Two marks cheaper. It was worth it.

But it turned out quite differently. He delivered the parcel, and asked at the same time whether they had any chocolate.

'Yes, there's a new line just in. It only costs seven marks as well. Fritz can have it for five marks, tell him.'

'Can I take a block now?'

'Have you got the money? We only sell for cash.'

Peter nodded, pulled out a note, and paid for the chocolate. He ran down the street feeling tremendously relieved. He hadn't needed to tell a fib. He was so pleased about it that he forgot to keep his wits about him.

Suddenly he found himself surrounded by a chain of policemen. They had rounded up a number of others too. He tried to dodge under the arms of two of them, but without success. He was held with the others, who were equally surprised by the sudden police raid. They were pushed on to a lorry.

'Throw your stuff away,' he heard one man say to his neighbour.

'I've only got cash in my pocket.'

'Drop it anyway. You've probably got quite a bit.'

The second man nodded. 'An empty pocket's safer anyway.'

Peter's mind was in a whirl. Would his black-market chocolate be taken off him? Would he be put in prison because of it? What would happen? Would there be questioning? What about these grumbling, swearing men in the lorry with him? Should he throw it away? Gisela's chocolate?

Pray!

The thought flashed through his mind. Was it possible to pray about something like this?

After all, he had bought it and paid for it in the proper way. He hadn't told any lies. Gisela was so ill, and he only wanted it for Gisela, and just now he had been thrilled that he had been able to get it so easily and cheaply. Well, cheap by today's standards, anyway.

The lorry stopped. The police took good care that nobody escaped. Peter marched with the others, his head down, into the big grey building.

The people were sorted out in a long corridor. Peter

stood facing a policeman who was so tall and broad that Peter was completely dwarfed beside him.

'Well, youngster, what have you got? Turn out your pockets.'

Without a word the boy pulled out the chocolate.

'Is that all?'

'It's for Gisela.'

'I see, for Gisela. Where did you get it?'

'I bought it.'

'Where?'

Silence.

'Come on, tell me.'

Silence.

'Take it off him, the stubborn urchin,' said a voice in the background.

Peter didn't dare look round.

'It's for Gisela. She has been very ill and has a craving for some chocolate. I paid five marks for it.' He spoke hoarsely.

He felt himself being grasped firmly and painfully by the ear.

'So! It's for Gisela. Who is this Gisela?'

Peter turned round to face the speaker. 'She's in hospital in East Street.'

'I see, in hospital. You know, I only have to ring up to find out whether you're telling the truth. And if you're not . . .'

Peter's eyes lit up. 'Yes, you ring up. Gisela Fehling. First of all she was in the little room, by herself, and now she's in the big ward.'

The man with the broad shoulders laughed.

'All right. You seem to be telling the truth. Shall we let him go?'

The other nodded. 'But don't let us catch you again, understand?'

Peter ran off as fast as his legs could carry him.

He didn't tell Gisela anything about his brush with the police when he visited her on the Sunday. Her beaming face, the grateful squeeze of her hand and her general pleasure more than made up for the episode. But a certain amount of fear still remained in his heart. What would happen if he were caught with one of Fritz and Alfred's parcels? How would that look? If the police unwrapped one of those parcels, he wouldn't get off as lightly as he had done with Gisela's chocolate.

I must take much more care, he kept thinking.

Gisela's condition improved every day. Each time Peter went she would smile in welcome. Soon he began to find her in a deck-chair on the terrace. She always asked after Peps. Peter made excuses. Peps was too dirty to come into a hospital.

'But you'll be coming out soon, Gisela, and then you'll see Peps. Then we'll be able to go home together straight-away. I've been earning money, and I've saved it all, so that we can go by train.'

He didn't tell her anything about the travel permits, or the frontier.

'Peter, I'm so glad I've got you. How pleased Mummy will be when we arrive. Sometimes when I can't get to sleep at night it's very quiet, and I can see the stars from my bed. Then I think about Mummy and wonder where she is, and whether she's waiting for me. And then I remember that she doesn't know where I am. And I can't write her a letter because I haven't got the address. Sometimes I cry a bit. Is that awful?'

Peter shook his head. 'Of course not, why should it be?'

'Well, that time when we first met, you said I was brave not to cry. I remember exactly, that's what you said. But now?'

'Oh, you mustn't worry about that. Especially when you've been so ill. It's such a long time since you were separated from your mother, and I can't be with you all the time now either.'

'It will be super to go by train. We'll get there quite quickly then. I don't know whether I could walk all that far now. My legs have got so thin, I can't even stand for long.'

'They'll get better soon. You'll be here for a while yet. Then, when you can walk, you can just come to us, to our flat. It isn't a proper flat, but you'll be able to sleep there till I've got the tickets.'

Another time Gisela wanted to know exactly where Peter was living.

'I'll explain it to you. It's quite near here. All the houses have been bombed. Almost the whole street. When you go out of the front door you must turn left. Do you know which is left?'

'Of course! The opposite hand to the one I write with!'

'Fine. Well, that's the way you must go. It's quite a good idea for you to know. Perhaps you could just come when you find you can walk properly again.'

'Oh, I can't just walk out. That wouldn't do. Besides, I don't know where my clothes are. The things I've got on now don't belong to me. But go on—turn left, and then?'

'First of all you come to a corner. You'll see that there was a street there once, but now there are only bombed houses. But at the next corner you must turn left again. There's a wall there. It's got "Baker" written on it. You can still read it quite clearly. That's where you go in—you can see that there used to be a door there. When you've climbed over the pile of rubble—it's not high, Peps can manage it quite easily—you'll see a little yard. Then you just climb down, and you'll find where we live. It probably used to be a wash-kitchen. Why don't you come with me straightaway now?'

The nurse appeared with the tray. Gisela beckoned to her.

'Nurse, when can I go home with Peter? I'm already much better.'

'Don't you like it here any more?'

'Oh, yes, but I must go to Mummy some time.'

'I didn't think you knew where she was. Where will you stay until we've found her?'

'I've got enough money. We're going to travel to

Düsseldorf together,' Peter said with pride, although rather self-consciously.

The nurse gave the boy a long, hard look. Then she stroked Gisela's hair.

'You must be patient, Gisela. We must discuss it with the doctor first. If he gives permission, you'll soon be able to go to your mother.'

Peter realized only too well that she was trying to put them off. She had looked so strangely at him. What were they planning to do with Gisela? He glowered.

Gisela felt for his hand and said quietly, 'Don't be sad, Peter. When they let me go from here I'll come straight to you, I promise. I can't just run away, especially when they've looked after me for such a long time.'

'If you promise that you'll come straight to us.'

The girl nodded earnestly. 'Yes, I promise.'

'I hope it's soon.' Peter gave her his hand and left.

Gisela is now getting better and is receiving special care. Peter has succeeded in getting them half way to Düsseldorf and Peps has kept out of trouble.

But this is not all that happens to three children.

Read about their next adventures in The Wrong Train, *Tiger Book, price 5s.*